"We are confronted with a historic choi[ce] nationalism, misogyny, homophobia, and xenophobia, or moving forward as a multicultural society built on mutual respect, equality, and the widest possible participation in shaping better social arrangements. Kim and del Prado, in a gentle, loving tone that encourages honesty, empathy, and risk-taking, provide much-needed counsel as well as attainable steps that will greatly help us transcend what divides us, grow fulfilling personal relationships, and advance the struggle for social justice. *It's Time to Talk (and Listen)* is extremely wise and entirely timely."

> —**Terry A. Kupers, MD, MSP**, professor emeritus in the department of psychology at The Wright Institute in Berkeley, CA, and author of *Solitary*

"*It's Time to Talk (and Listen)* deals with clashes in cultural values, incivility, interpersonal conflicts, and communication difficulties. The authors, Anatasia Kim and Alicia del Prado, have written an impressive guide to overcoming the dilemmas experienced by people in an increasingly diverse and varied environment. Through personal examples, case studies, and cognitive behavioral notions, they outline tools to enhance one's well-being and functioning. Step-by-step exercises and lessons are presented that clearly outline a systematic way to help oneself. The book is straightforward, engaging, and sensible. It has the potential for improving the lives of those who want to more effectively function in our diverse society."

> —**Stanley Sue, PhD**, distinguished professor emeritus at Palo Alto University, and distinguished professor emeritus at University of California, Davis

"At a time when our country is more polarized than ever, with deeply felt traumas, fears, and pain preventing us from empathizing with opposing viewpoints, Anatasia Kim and Alicia del Prado's intentional approach to bridging these divides is vital. In *It's Time to Talk (and Listen)*, the authors rightly emphasize the need to attend to one's own emotional reactions, and to allow for an openness to another's truth. With this, they bring hope for a more just, less divided, and more authentically connected society."

> —**Monika Parikh, MA, MP**[A] [...]t of Partnerships for Trauma

"This is a must-read for anyone wanting to have productive conversations about culture and diversity. Kim and del Prado provide a step-by-step approach to engaging in 'constructive conversations,' using the Kim Constructive Conversations Model. This book is perfect for anyone who has struggled to manage awkward, possibly offensive comments at the dinner table, on the airplane, or in the office. A superb and timely contribution given the current sociopolitical climate."

> —**Claytie Davis III, PhD, ABPP**, director of training at the
> University of California, Berkeley, and chair-elect of the Association
> of Psychology Postdoctoral and Internship Centers (APPIC)

"It was a pleasure to read this timely book, in which Kim and del Prado provide a thoughtful and practical framework for respectful, value-driven, and compassionate conversations about culture, diversity, oppression, and privilege. Blending theory, research, and engaging vignettes, the authors delineate a concrete and self-reflective approach for constructive dialogue that empowers us to participate in an authentic manner with diverse others about salient yet divisive topics. Doing so will deepen our understanding of other people, encourage us to embrace differences, facilitate individual and collective healing, foster genuine and close relationships, and lay the groundwork for greater equity and inclusivity."

> —**Nadine J. Kaslow, PhD, ABPP**, professor and chief psychologist
> at Emory University School of Medicine, and past president of
> the American Psychological Association

"Kim and del Prado are to be commended for their book, which represents the best of George Miller's call to 'give psychology away.' They have provided a practical, step-by-step guide to difficult conversations regarding culture, race, and ethnicity. Using key principles derived from multicultural psychology, they have created a highly accessible guide grounded in the exploration of each user's values, motives, and needs. This book should be studied by anyone who is interested in promoting constructive dialogues with coworkers, friends, acquaintances, and neighbors on potentially divisive topics. It is a very timely contribution given the current schisms within our society."

> —**Frederick Leong, PhD**, professor in the department of psychology
> and psychiatry, and director of the consortium for multicultural
> psychology research at Michigan State University

"Bravo to Kim and del Prado for clearly laying out pragmatic steps to navigate difficult conversations. This is a very timely book given the current sociopolitical context.... Their model gives us hope that we can cross multiple divides to see the humanity in others."

—**Steven R. Lopez, PhD**, professor in the department of psychology and social work at the University of Southern California

"I admire and respect the intentions behind Anatasia Kim and Alicia del Prado's *It's Time to Talk (and Listen)*. Constructive conversations about difficult topics are, by definition, very hard to have. Kim and del Prado, in my opinion, treat the ability to have such conversations as a skill that can be learned. The Kim Constructive Conversations Model revolves around the topics of culture and diversity, but the actual model can also be applied broadly to other challenging topics—subjects that we often avoid. Perhaps the most important takeaway for me, after reading this text, was the authors' heartfelt belief that we can make difficult and painful situations better, especially surrounding diverging views on culture and diversity. And we can do this by following a model of sorts, one that is grounded in our own values and integrity. Thank you Anatasia and Alicia, for sharing your thoughts, suggested instruction, and explicit bias that we can all improve the way we deal with difficult topics."

—**David M. Lechuga, PhD**, UCLA-trained clinical psychologist, former president of the California Psychological Association (CPA) and the Hispanic Neuropsychological Society, and current chair of the CPA's Division of Neuropsychology

"Kim and del Prado create a safe space to examine one's authentic self without first having to apologize for gender, ethnicity, identity, cultural norms, or economic status. In doing so, the reader is invited to journey inward, and peel away layers of self by identifying intentions, exposing obstacles, and clarifying principles that inform how we act on or react to conversations that may make us uncomfortable. It is through the examination of the nuanced self, that the authors are then able to guide the reader on a path to constructive communication with others."

—**Irene St. Roseman, EdD**, cofounder/head of school, Oxford Day Academy

"For too long, dialogues on multicultural issues turn to debates, trying to prove why each person is right in their respective positions. What I love most about Kim and del Prado's book is the use of their own lives to illustrate their eight-step approach, while situating ALL readers to examine our own 'stuff' as we attempt to honor ourselves while listening to others. The book is practical, with case examples and reflective exercises that can be used by anyone. I love the book's capacity to serve as a model for constructive conversations both within and outside academia. It is accessible, and while an easy read, they challenge us to look beyond simple solutions to difficult dialogues. Not an easy task, but a necessary one if we are to truly affirm the humanity in others."

—**Miguel E. Gallardo, PsyD**, professor in the department of
psychology; and program director of Aliento, The Center for
Latina/o Communities at Pepperdine University

"Kim and del Prado's *It's Time to Talk (and Listen)* is timely, important, and urgently needed. At a time when so many Americans feel divided by issues that intersect with race and diversity, it offers hope and invites opportunities for healing through practical, step-by-step guidance on how to talk about and understand each other as well as our differences. The powerful stories and thought-provoking exercises embedded throughout the text promote deep personal reflection, astute self-awareness, genuine understanding, and purposeful action and change. Everyone can benefit from this book."

—**Rachel N. Casas, PhD**, associate professor in the graduate
department of psychology at California Lutheran University

"I'm ashamed to admit how many friends I've unfriended, blocked, or muted on social media because I couldn't have a conversation with them about our differences. I wish *It's Time to Talk (and Listen)* had been published sooner. Its practical approach to understanding who you are, sharing what's important to you, and listening to others helped me take a more courageous path forward instead of impulsively avoiding people I disagree with. Kim and del Prado have created a wonderful resource for anyone interested in navigating the polarized minefield of our everyday lives."

—**Ali Mattu, PhD**, clinical psychologist and assistant professor
at Columbia University Irving Medical Center, and host of
The Psych Show on YouTube

"Simultaneously practical and scholarly, this splendid book provides the outstanding eight-step Kim Constructive Conversations Model, to deal with contentious, complex topics that often contain emotional minefields, especially about culture and diversity. Kim and del Prado acknowledge our unfathomably deep collective wounds across hundreds of years, as well as the ongoing experiences of being ignored, dismissed, neglected, avoided, or invalidated. Conversations about difficult, painful topics are not only important, but in certain contexts, can be a moral responsibility! The model provides an opportunity to go through those experiences in bold and courageous ways, which can lead to a place of clarity, grace, and compassion for oneself and others. This inspiring guide is a treasure that can provide direction, grounding, and comfort for anyone who experiences microaggressions, and their allies."

—**Melba J. T. Vasquez, PhD, ABPP**, independent practice
in Austin, TX, and former president of the American
Psychological Association

"Kim and del Prado have written a welcoming, engaging, and much-needed book! Their approach makes having potentially explosive conversations seem less daunting and possible, while still remaining true to the nuances and complexities of such conversations. *It's Time to Talk (and Listen)* is a must-read for everyone, especially during these unprecedented times, as we all collectively grapple with some of the most uncomfortable, distressing, and painful issues that have been plaguing our society and our psyche."

—**E.J.R. David, PhD**, associate professor in the department
of psychology at the University of Alaska Anchorage, and
author of *We Have Not Stopped Trembling Yet* and *Brown Skin,
White Minds*

"Kim and del Prado present timely, tested, and immediately applicable methods for interpersonal understanding and repair. A valuable tool for families, institutions, and communities during this divisive and stressful era."

—**Helen H. Hsu, PsyD**, president of the Asian American
Psychological Association, and staff psychologist at
Stanford University

"I'll be introducing this practical and expert guide to our organization because it supports difficult conversations about experiences of diverse oppression in a way that prioritizes mutual respect, relationship connections, and finding common ground. The authors' inclusion of their personal experiences encourages humility, vulnerability, and courage in the process."

—**Megan Kirshbaum, PhD**, founder and executive director of
Through the Looking Glass, and director of The National
Center for Parents with Disabilities and Their Families

"Presenting a practical and accessible eight-step model on how to participate in constructive dialogues about issues of culture and diversity, the authors utilize multiple examples and invite readers to participate, reflect, and journal in a tone that is conversational and approachable. The emphasis on talking with, rather than talking at, others from a place of personal awareness and growth is emphasized throughout. This book is a useful resource for individuals across disciplines and professional contexts who are interested in participating in dialogues that can promote greater mutual understanding, and even healing, related to difficult cultural topics."

—**Cirleen DeBlaere, PhD**, associate professor in the department
of counseling psychology at Georgia State University, and
coauthor of *Cultural Humility*

IT'S TIME TO TALK (AND LISTEN)

HOW TO HAVE
CONSTRUCTIVE
CONVERSATIONS
ABOUT RACE, CLASS,
SEXUALITY, ABILITY
& GENDER IN A
POLARIZED WORLD

ANATASIA S. KIM, PhD
ALICIA DEL PRADO, PhD

New Harbinger Publications, Inc.

Publisher's Note

In consideration of evolving American English usage standards, and reflecting a commitment to equity for all genders, "they/them" is used in this book to denote singular persons.

Distributed in Canada by Raincoast Books

Copyright © 2019 by Anatasia S. Kim and Alicia del Prado
New Harbinger Publications, Inc.
5674 Shattuck Avenue
Oakland, CA 94609
www.newharbinger.com

Cover design by Amy Shoup

Acquired by Ryan Buresh

Edited by Teja Watson

Text design by Michele Waters and Tracy Carlson

Library of Congress Cataloging-in-Publication Data on file

Printed in the United States of America

21   20   19

10   9   8   7   6   5   4   3   2   1   First Printing

To Dexter and Serena,
my endlessly patient and generous teachers,
and to Quincy, my everything.

—Anatasia S. Kim

To my sons, Ethan and Mason, who inspire me every day,
and who slept on my lap while I typed many of these pages.

—Alicia M. del Prado

CONTENTS

FOREWORD

As a scholar-activist, I frequently initiate uncomfortable conversations about race, gender, sexuality, class, ethnicity, and religion. In psychology courses where I teach about social justice and systemic oppression, I regularly facilitate difficult dialogues exploring students' biases and pointing out racial, gendered, and cultural classroom dynamics. As a consultant and multicultural "fixer," I am often invited to workplaces or college campuses after "incidents" occur, where I facilitate dialogues on how colleagues can improve intercultural communication or provide trainings on how to manage implicit biases and microaggressions. Even in my everyday life, I commonly find myself asking people, "What did you mean by that?" when they make microaggressive comments about me, my family, or my work.

Despite these experiences, I could not tell you when I first started willfully engaging in difficult dialogues, nor how I learned to navigate them. As a teenager, I heard many hurtful jokes related to race, gender, and sexuality; yet, I can't recall ever speaking up against them. In college, while racial tensions reverberated all over campus and led to avoidance and segregation, professors or administrators hardly addressed them or made us talk. In graduate school, where I typically was the only Filipino American and the only queer person (and often the only person of color), I constantly debated whether to participate in classroom discussions, in fear of having to represent all of the members of my groups, or of having to protect myself from being invalidated, dismissed, or gaslit.

One reason why I entered academia was to improve the ways that multiculturalism was integrated into teaching, research, and scholarship. I wanted to provide the next generation of multicultural psychologists with academic literature that validated my own lived experiences while normalizing people who are usually "othered." I wanted to educate people with privileged identities on how systemic oppression influences all of us, and I wanted to create spaces (in classrooms, in workplaces, in clinical settings, and in homes) where people could talk, listen, and learn from each other.

Early in my career, I picked up on many common dynamics that made multicultural teaching emotionally exhausting. While all individuals generally can become defensive, they do so for different reasons. People from privileged groups often describe feeling "attacked" when confronted on the ways they are complicit to systemic oppression. People of historically marginalized groups often shut down out of exhaustion or frustration, or to protect themselves from being hurt further. As a facilitator, I ordinarily navigate a rollercoaster of emotions—feeling triggered when participants question my abilities; drained when conflicts emerge; and defeated when people just didn't seem to "get it." While I am fortunate to have mentors and colleagues to debrief or process each situation, my wounds took time to heal, and my anxiety increased each time I entered the "battlefield" again.

It's Time to Talk (And Listen): How to Have Constructive Conversations About Race, Class, Sexuality, Ability & Gender in a Polarized World successfully identifies and normalizes the psychological and emotional processes of engaging in conversations that people tend to avoid or dread. In naming the anxieties that people have in even *thinking* about issues deemed taboo or too political, Drs. Anatasia Kim and Alicia del Prado provide crucial reassurance and guidance for each aspect of the process. The heart of the book is the Kim Constructive Conversations Model—a guide to approaching dialogues about race, gender, sexuality, and other identities. Moving beyond the "courageous" conversation to a "constructive" one, the authors highlight an array of practical strategies and tools—from identifying a grounded goal to locating and acknowledging barriers.

The authors encourage self-reflection throughout—inviting readers to journal and challenging them to identify their emotional triggers or blind spots. They provide case studies and exercises which assist readers in gaining (or increasing) self-awareness, particularly about their own implicit biases or problematic internalized notions. The authors take their own "turns" in sharing personal reflections— proving not only that they practice what they preach, but also modeling how to emotionally navigate constructive conversations themselves. Through their own personal voices and narratives, the authors also emphasize healing and self-care—qualities that are critical when engaging in social justice work and addressing cultural traumas.

Further, Kim and del Prado push readers to consider the perspectives of others who are different from them. Still acknowledging the role of systemic oppression, people of historically marginalized groups are validated in their rights to be angry or frustrated, *and* are also encouraged to move beyond (or through) those emotions. Such nuances are important, as people of historically marginalized groups (e.g., people of color, women, LGBTQ people) are often tasked with the responsibility (or burden) of teaching multiculturalism, in ways that makes people of privileged groups (e.g., white people, men, heterosexuals) feel comfortable. The authors' push for people with privilege to take initiative in sharing the burden of multicultural learning is refreshing and validating.

Perhaps one of the greatest "take home" messages for me is the importance for readers to reflect upon why they experience their emotions and what those emotions may mask. People of privileged groups often feel defensive and tense—which likely protect their feelings of guilt and shame. People of historically marginalized groups tend to turn to anger, frustration, or resentment—which likely protect hurt, trauma, and internalized oppression. People with both privileged and less privileged identities navigate both simultaneously (e.g., white women who feel guilty about their whiteness and frustration and sadness about sexism), which further complicate their emotional processes. Identifying and managing these primary emotions is imperative for engaging in constructive conversations, but also for surviving and thriving in life.

It's Time to Talk (and Listen) should be required for educators, therapists, employers, and supervisors, as well as students, clients, employees, and supervisees. It provides the tools that are needed for people to better understand themselves, which will allow them to better understand others and to communicate more effectively. In a time in which our society is more polarized than it perhaps has ever been, it is finally time for us to talk (and to listen) in real, organic, and meaningful ways. I commend Drs. Kim and del Prado for arming us with the strategies and tools to help survive the battlefields ahead.

—Kevin L. Nadal, PhD
City University of New York

PREFACE

Have you ever been in a conversation in which someone's speech or behavior is culturally offensive? Maybe at your place of work, at the dinner table, on a blind date, at the supermarket, during a basketball game, or even during a job interview?

In this scenario, what, if anything, did you do? For many of us, "nothing" is an all too familiar answer to this question. You probably fantasized about what you would, could, or should have said. Maybe you even promised yourself that the next time you *will* open your mouth. Don't worry, you're not alone. Whether at work or at home, on the subway or during a family dinner, situations like this have become more and more commonplace and complex.

In recent years, the call for difficult dialogues about controversial issues has increased. But how? It is not uncommon these days for family members with different political opinions to stop speaking to each other after exchanging mutually offensive words. It's also typical for people to completely avoid discussing important topics altogether, anticipating the inevitable conflict. And if the situation happens at less than ideal times and places, say when you're running late or at work, these excuses make avoidance even easier. If silence sits at one end of the continuum and verbal conflict at the other, how do we reach a middle ground? How do we respectfully come together so that both parties can speak and listen?

This book is about having constructive conversations regarding culture and diversity. The Kim Constructive Conversations Model is a step-by-step approach that is grounded in a commitment to healing and to honoring your personal values. Broaching cultural topics can help heal the legacy of trauma, silence, and shame by moving toward intimacy in a relationship that embraces differences. We believe that highlighting healing in this model is important, as we must aspire to individually and collectively tend to our wounds. Through continuous and persistent constructive conversations, we believe this is possible.

It will certainly not happen overnight. It is an investment. A serious commitment. But certainly one worth making to ourselves and each other.

The Kim Constructive Conversations Model will teach you to engage in effective, candid, and compassionate conversations with family, friends, colleagues, and even strangers about any controversial topic, including racism, immigration, sexism, all-gender restrooms, marriage equality, gun violence, reproductive rights, classism, religious differences, ableism, marginalization, and more.

We believe that constructive conversations about culture and diversity can be for everybody. *All* people, despite internal and external challenges, can engage courageously and effectively on important matters critical to our collective well-being. Family members, CEOs of Fortune 500 companies, supervisors and their employees, staff with their managers, patrons at a coffee shop, college students in sororities and fraternities, actors and directors on their sets…the possibilities are endless. This book is not intended for people from any particular cultural group or political outlook. Rather, constructive conversations can be used by all who are willing and open to engaging.

Imagine you are at a baseball game. An elderly fan in front of you yells at the Korean pitcher to "go back home!"

Your blood starts to boil, and you yell at the man, "Shut up! You can't say that!" He turns around a little surprised and says, "What?!" You quickly and loudly shout, "That's racist!" with a clear intent to emphatically shut him down.

While in this scenario you may be calling out a blatant macro-aggression, this verbal confrontation is *not* a constructive conversation. Why not? After all, you confronted racism head-on. And in this day and age, isn't this what we need?

Yes! We strongly believe that racism and macroaggressions need to be called out for what they are, and we hope that you can and will do this. It takes tremendous courage and quite a bit of energy, but it is a must in order to combat the social diseases of prejudice and discrimination.

Many great leaders have spoken directly, swiftly, and loudly when naming injustice. It is empowering and even healing to voice one's mind with clarity and undoctored truthfulness. However, "that's racist," in and of itself, is not a constructive conversation. What we're talking about here is not a "one and done" model. Instead, a truly constructive conversation is one that involves all parties talking, listening, and communicating collaboratively.

Kim Constructive Conversations Model: Practical Steps

What is a constructive conversation? A constructive conversation is an exchange in which the people involved speak about their personal experiences, thoughts, feelings, and beliefs on matters of culture and diversity, and listen to the other person with genuine openness.

In his book *Courageous Conversations About Race: A Field Guide for Achieving Equity in Schools* (2015), Glenn E. Singleton writes that a courageous conversation on race engages those who won't talk, sustains dialogue even if it gets uncomfortable, and enhances communication such that deep understanding and meaningful actions occur.

By contrast, the Kim Constructive Conversations Model is a step-by-step guide to conversations about culture and diversity. The how-to includes understanding and successfully managing both external and internal processes in potentially emotion-charged situations. To date, much emphasis has been placed on external processes, such as content, word choices, or rules of engagement that focus on the overt and concrete dialogue between those attempting to engage about culture and diversity. Though certainly important, focusing simply on the external process unfortunately fails to capture the full story and experience. As such, the Kim Constructive Conversations Model expands on existing frameworks to include the subtler, and arguably the more important, internal process. Focusing internally on factors such as our personality, emotional reactions, goals, and values, and developing useful skills from this place of self-reflection and self-understanding, can exponentially enhance the success of difficult dialogues on culture and diversity. This is turn makes it easier to take risks, even when emotions are strong, stakes high, and outcomes uncertain.

In the 8-step Kim Constructive Conversations Model, healing is emphasized. As Singleton suggests, this involves a commitment to genuine understanding and meaningful action. This means that the intention in having constructive conversations is not merely for external motives—to patch up an occasional misunderstanding or smooth out a few ruffled feathers in order to gain others' approval or avoid future social faux pas. Rather, there is a clear and deliberate wish to be impacted deeply and purposefully—to be changed inside and out.

Consider people with cancer. Survivors know that the path to healing is fraught with challenges big and small. As they heal—from surgery, chemotherapy, or radiation—it doesn't always feel good. In fact, they often feel much worse before they get better. Oncologists know they need to be direct and honest about the difficulties that lay ahead. They know that the strength of the patient's character, courage, and resolve will play just as profound a role in their healing as the treatments they will receive.

The disease of oppression is no different. In order to heal from injustice, in order to have constructive conversations, you must be strong and brave. You must accept that the journey will not always be easy, and you will certainly not feel good all the time.

But just as with a cancer patient, the alternative—not seeking treatment—is too precarious. It means allowing the disease to eventually take over.

Oppression and injustice too will take over if we do nothing. Just because the path to healing is long, uncertain, and difficult does not mean we give up before starting. As we slowly move forward, one constructive conversation at a time, our capacity to understand deeply and undertake meaningful actions will strengthen. And as we have noted, constructive conversations have boundless potential for healing.

So how do you practice this? The book that follows will help you move beyond lip service and show you *how* to speak from the heart with tools from the head. Emphasis is placed on not just why, what, and when we speak, but more important, on understanding *how* we talk with one another. You will learn tools that are supported by research and have been practiced in classrooms, work meetings, therapy rooms, and even around dinner tables.

The 8-step model is straightforward and easy to follow. With practice, the steps will become second nature and you will see your skills improve. They will help you focus, stay in the moment, and verbalize your thoughts and feelings, while also being open to the other person's perspective.

In Step 1, you identify your goal. In Step 2, you acknowledge the barriers to engaging in a given constructive conversation. In Step 3, you address any barriers by creating a value-driven intention. Next, you set the stage (Step 4), and then you take action (Step 5). In Step 6, you invite, listen, and process the receiver's response. In Step 7, you acknowledge, reflect, and respond to the receiver's reactions. And in Step 8, you repeat and do it again.

As you can see from these steps, a constructive conversation is not a one-sided lecture or monologue. Rather, it's a thoughtful and reciprocal connection, intended to deepen mutual understanding and ultimately lead to change.

How It All Started

We are both passionate about the world of multicultural psychology. We've taught classes, held trainings, and even organized national conferences on the subject. However, issues pertaining to culture and diversity continue to be among the most challenging topics to converse about. For years, our students and colleagues have told us that they struggle with how to effectively talk about these topics in classroom discussions.

They are not alone! We frequently get questions like, "What do I actually say?" and "How do I bring it up?" We too have had our own struggles, both at work and in our personal lives, when trying to address culture and diversity issues that are important to us. It is from this struggle that the 8-step model was born.

As we are psychologists who work from a cognitive behavioral background, it's no surprise that the model is grounded in a practical, linear approach of goal-setting, self-assessment, collaborative dialogue, and personal values. We try to break things down to their simplest parts so that readers have the ABCs of how to engage about culture and diversity.

We define "culture" and "diversity" broadly and inclusively. Culture includes but is not necessarily limited to race, ethnicity, gender, sexual identity, class, ability, spirituality, religion, and age. Additional layers of cultural complexity also include geographic location of origin, level of educational attainment, marital status, relationship status, diverse family structures, political identity, and veteran status or military affiliation. Our conceptualization of diversity includes the understanding that our identities and experiences are heterogeneous and variegated. It's also crucial that we respect and honor how we each have multiple, intersecting identities. The use of culture and diversity also acknowledges the reality of inequity, the harmful impacts of unexamined privilege, and the overwhelming injustices in our global society, including all forms of discrimination, such as racism, colorism, sexism, heterosexism, classism, ableism, xenophobia, and ageism.

After many years of talking about these steps in workshops and at conferences, we finally decided to take the leap and write the approach all down. So here we are!

Meet Anatasia Kim, PhD

The 8-step model was born some years ago for the sole purpose of serving one person—me. I remember precisely the moment when the steps came to me. I was taking an unusually early evening shower. (Yes, shower epiphanies do happen!) I had been struggling for some weeks to stay motivated at work. There had been numerous heated conversations among faculty and graduate students around if and how to teach multicultural studies. It was intense, necessary, and, frankly, a long time coming.

But I was feeling depleted and demoralized. I questioned whether I could hold on for the long haul. I feared I didn't have enough in my reserve. I feared what I might say or do. I was also afraid I might simply walk away. I even started looking for another job. I was a serious flight risk.

Of course, what was happening at work was nothing surprising or new. In fact, it was something I usually welcome—open, direct, no-BS talk. We were finally talking honestly about the herd of elephants in the room. Should multiculturalism be taught experientially? Are we traumatizing our students by asking them to deeply examine their privilege and internalized oppression? Is such learning unduly burdensome for more privileged students? Shouldn't they be protected as well? Maybe we should just vote to eliminate the course altogether given that it seems to be creating so much emotionality and strife in the school? These issues were not unique to our program; they were challenges for many social science doctoral programs across the country.

But for a myriad of reasons, these discussions really got to me. This work was important and way too personal. I was not about to go down without a fight. But I realized that what was depleting my energy and hope was an uncomfortable feeling. Pain. I was deeply hurt, my spirit wounded.

Like so many people, I have had my share of experiences with cultural oppression. The uncomfortable yet eerily familiar feeling of pain came flooding back from a past I had kept locked away. Growing up as a young immigrant child in Southern California—with limited economic resources, community violence, and rampant racism—left an indelible impression on me. I learned very quickly to not ask questions, to not challenge stereotypes or authority, to smile and nod. All this while my identity was constantly cross-examined, my pride perpetually bruised, and my heart aching to scream back.

But silence and inaction ruled; I learned very early that challenging the status quo was to be avoided at all cost. My attempts at practicing the perfect rebuttals or threats, no matter how clever, always fell short. Reporting on others' misbehaviors also came with the heavy price of alienation or the stark possibility of retaliation. The temporary satisfaction of a good comeback, even when it worked, retreated as quickly as it had appeared. Change and justice felt like wasted hope, a useless fantasy. But giving up was also not an option.

I desperately wanted to be brave. I wanted to stand up—to everyone. To my father, who allowed police officers to talk down to him. To the doctors and store clerks, who assumed my family's social class and treated us accordingly. And even to my peers, who projected their own internalized racism onto me.

Fear and pain are difficult things to hold for a young person, especially for a long time. Whether we like it or not, they can and do wound us.

If you knew my mother, you'd know that the women in my family don't do wounded. The women of Jeju Island suck it up and march forward boldly, unapologetically. No time for crying and licking wounds. You get louder, stronger, and you push through. Hard.

This had been my operating mode for most of my adult life. It was especially the case when it came to multiculturalism and social justice—the very reasons I had pursued a graduate degree. I had no time for pain. There was work to be done.

But as much as I tried, I couldn't shake the gnawing pain. So I apprehensively turned toward it. I needed to do something. Even with a PhD, this was too difficult. I was coming undone. I desperately needed something to anchor me. The tornado of emotions was growing stronger and I was certain if left untethered, I would spiral out and say or do something I would later regret.

The 8 steps came to me in a matter of minutes. I've been trained as a cognitive behavioral therapist, so a step-by-step approach was both familiar and grounding. I knew I needed to slow myself down so that whatever I said or did would come from a place of clarity and intention. I also needed to create space for the pain. But how? As someone who treats anxiety, I knew that I needed to turn toward, and not away from, the fear of that pain. My spiritual practice in Buddhism and my study on the neuroscience of Buddhist psychology also proved to be invaluable influences. I was reminded that in order to find enlightenment and liberation, I must first look within and begin to understand the source of my pain and suffering. This framework became an important foundation for the model.

So the constructive conversations model was born that early evening, against the backdrop of my children outside the bathroom door asking when dinner would be ready. It gave me something to hold on to as I committed to bravely and humbly turn toward and soften into the pain and suffering.

It was clear that the solution was not to avoid or run and get another job, or even to reactively end relationships, which I'd been known to do. Instead, I needed to stay, to face my fear and anger. I needed to unmute, to listen, and to connect deeply, honestly, and compassionately.

So, I committed to opening my heart, still raw and vulnerable. I committed to doing my part to lessen the great chasm between "us" and "them," to work *with* and not only against or in spite of others. The steps gave me a game plan; the values, especially of faith and courage, gave me important tools. In the years that followed, as I collaborated with Alicia and began to practice the model myself, I realized that I could be both unwavering in my pursuit of social justice and also hold deeply to mercy and grace for myself and others. In so doing, I could speak boldly and listen deeply. I could also hope and even heal.

I hope the Kim Constructive Conversations Model will help you too, in your endeavors to transform yourself and those around you. Our collective wounds are unfathomably deep, having traveled with us across hundreds of years. The pain we have inflicted is incalculable. Yet we have too often ignored, dismissed, neglected, avoided, invalidated, and danced around the untold atrocities of past and present. We must stop this—together.

Now is the time to start connecting, talking, listening, and healing. It's long overdue. We owe it to ourselves. We owe it to those whose shoulders we stand on. And most urgently, we owe it to those who will inherit our collective legacy, our children.

Meet Alicia del Prado, PhD

From an early age, I knew I was loved, but also that I was different from the family that loved me. One of the most influential people in my life is my Italian American grandfather, John Salvatore Provenzale. This tall, slender man with white hair and a booming voice was Nonno to me. And Nonno (Italian for "grandfather") knew how to make me, his brown-skinned, multiracial granddaughter of divorced parents, feel important, worthy, and beautiful.

Nonno was also a traditional and conservative man, and I imagine if he was alive today he and I would not see eye to eye on some things, or likely many things! That being said, my love for him is strong and true, and I am confident that having a white man play such a positive role in my life influences my genuine desire to have constructive conversations with people who look and are so different from me.

From an early age, I pronounced with certainty to my classmates that I was "Filipino, Italian, Spanish, and Chinese." These were the identity terms that my parents and grandparents taught me, and I quickly made them my own. During my childhood, I became very equipped to thrive in a variety of different social situations, and I was capable of interacting and getting along with people from a range of different backgrounds.

I grew up in the San Francisco Bay Area with a large extended family, many of whom were Filipino, Italian, Salvadoran, Irish, Puerto Rican, and African American. Perhaps as a part of my family fabric, I had an innate desire to foster communication and bridge connections between different communities. These personal and family experiences influenced my decision to study cross-cultural psychology, as well as my ultimate career path as a counseling psychologist who loves helping and working with diverse groups of people.

I met Anatasia at the Wright Institute in Berkeley in 2008. We shared a passion for multiculturalism and social justice and soon became "sisters" in work and life. When Anatasia first shared with me the 8 steps she'd designed, I thought to myself, *This is genius!* It has been an honor to present, practice, and partner with Anatasia on the further development of these steps. We call each other when our practice of the 8 steps goes well. We also analyze together what went wrong when we're not satisfied with the constructive conversations we've embarked on.

In late 2017, I was on an airplane when a stranger sitting to the right of me asked, "You're on the left, right?" I was totally taken off guard. The woman speaking to me was a young white woman. Let's call her Tanya.

I hesitantly said yes when I registered that Tanya meant that I was on the political left. Tanya then proclaimed that she was "on the right" and continued to talk about topics that she had strong opinions about. Tanya shared her thoughts about Black Lives Matter, undocumented immigration, and also added that she thought Barack Obama was the "Antichrist."

I took a few deep breaths before replying. Not only have I owned two Obama T-shirts, I even had an Obama onesie for my newborn. For me, the election of Obama was personal and powerful for many reasons, but especially because I connected to his multiracial identity. He had a white mom. I have a white mom. His father was a man of color. My father is a man of color. I felt visible in the world in a way I hadn't felt before, and I had felt hopeful when Obama was in office. I wanted my children to partake in this hopeful future, where people of color could sometimes see themselves in their leadership.

After one more deep inhale, I began to disagree with Tanya. Despite the fact that she had been the one to initiate the conversation, Tanya seemed to feel uncomfortable as we got deeper into the issues. The dialogue was hard for both of us! During our talk, though, we also learned we had things in common, like both being mothers of young children. The plane eventually reached its destination, thank goodness, although the hours crept by slowly. Just prior to us getting off the plane, Tanya told me, "I appreciated our talk. Most people I talk to about this get upset, and it doesn't go so well."

I will never forget this conversation. I don't think either of us changed the other's mind, but it was the first constructive conversation I had with someone with very different views than my own since Trump was elected. It reminded me of the importance of dialogue, openness, and listening to others, even when we disagree. It would have been very easy for us to vilify each other. In fact, if I hadn't used the 8-step model, I probably would have been so caught off guard that I'd have been speechless, broken down and cried, or maybe even yelled. However, while still being true to myself and my opinions, I was also able to empathize with Tanya when she shared that she was bullied in school, and even to respect her when she shared about her life as a single mother.

I recount my experience on the plane to show how I truly believe in this model for constructive conversations. With a stranger that I disagreed with on pretty much every social and political topic, I was still able to be present in such a way that neither of us yelled, shut down completely, or pushed the call button for the flight attendant to change our seats. No emergency landing was needed. After all, we were both women, we were both mothers, we were both people with opinions and ideas who were willing to talk and listen to each other. We encountered each other in an authentic way, and I felt stronger and a little more whole afterward.

I believe that you can be genuine and can heal through conversations too.

How to Use This Book

We talk to people every day. Yet we often do it without thinking. This kind of speaking without forethought often leads to hurt feelings and fallings-out, especially when it comes to issues around culture and diversity. Lack of strategy and preparation doesn't make too much sense when you realize that communication is an art and a skill that we need no matter who we are. And as you well know, there are some things that feel impossibly too hard to talk about.

The Kim Constructive Conversations Model is meant to help well-meaning individuals like you who want clear instructions on how to have difficult dialogues about culture and diversity. It is also about the power of a good ear. Your desire to listen with sincerity, even for brief periods of time, can lead to amazing results. Deep listening is essential for constructive conversations.

This book should be used as a guide, to remind you about the gifts of imperfection, the importance of grounding and self-care, and the imperative of healing through connection. When you get lost or feel like giving up, we hope you can anchor yourself in any of the 8 steps. We all have areas of vulnerability, including fear of saying the wrong thing, of being misunderstood, of feeling alienated, or even of losing important relationships. We are all imperfect and fallible, even when we believe we are on the "right" side of an argument. In our own ways, we get overwhelmed by the enormity of the issues, the intensity of our emotions, and even the righteousness of our positions.

Pause however long you need. Then use the steps to continue and begin again. Taking care of yourself is more important than getting all the steps right. This is not a manual. We want you to use the steps in whatever ways you need, to remain steadfast in your commitment. Until you feel the seeds of your intentions sprouting and growing strong. The steps are here for you until you no longer feel like the only choices are to attack or hide.

You will not be alone on this journey. We will travel with you and guide you gently through every step. In sections we call "Your Turn," you will be asked to practice skills and to write and reflect in a journal of your own choosing. (Anything from a simple notebook from the dollar store to a fancy Moleskine will do—whatever is accessible and resonates best with you!) Having an active role in this process will prove invaluable to your learning and growth. We will also jump in periodically with our own personal anecdotes and experiences, in sections we call "Anatasia's Turn" and "Alicia's Turn." You will see firsthand that we are definitely in this with you!

We also advise you to recruit an accountability buddy, someone who is also committed to learning how to have constructive conversations about culture and diversity. Having someone with whom you can discuss, practice, and stay motivated will add extra support and motivation.

Finally, as you navigate through the book, remember to be yourself. We want you to be genuine in how you express yourself and naturally engage with others. At the same time, we encourage you to be open to trying new ways of connecting and communicating. Rather than invalidating the truth of who you are, trying new approaches and skills will allow you to communicate more effectively what you are truly seeking and needing. We will have solutions and tools for situations in which you may previously have felt silence was the only option.

Let us also be clear: While we think the importance of these types of conversations is pivotal, it does not mean that you can and should have them everywhere and all the time. The mere thought of constantly having such conversations is exhausting as well as unrealistic. There may also be many reasons not to engage—a history of abuse, violence, or other trauma with a particular person, for example.

That said, our goal is to teach a method for broaching and not avoiding conversations. We don't want you to burn out from too much talking and listening. Instead, we want you to not be afraid of the conversations. You are capable of engaging in them when you are ready, and this book will give you the tools you need, in order to know when and how.

Finally, we encourage you to keep in mind both short- and long-term goals. In the short term, you might commit to learning concrete tools and skills. In the long term, you might commit to staying the course. The overall goal is not about getting it right or doing it perfectly—there is no such thing! So as you find yourself being less than perfect, remember: You are not alone. We are all beautifully imperfect and fallible. This much we most certainly all have in common. Thank goodness!

MIRROR, MIRROR, ON THE WALL

Before we get started on the steps, let's first take a good look in the mirror. We vastly increase our chances of having healthy relationships with others if we have already done our own work on ourselves. Knowing ourselves honestly makes for greater relationship success.

So, the task for this introduction is to invite you to better understand yourself. Why are you reading this book? What are your expectations? What personality characteristics and skills might help or hinder you? What specific topics on culture and diversity are particularly challenging for you? And how might you best use this book?

In the following sections, we will invite you to address these important questions. This will serve as an important prerequisite to learning the step-by-step model.

Why Are You Reading This Book?

Did you pick up this book after a heated exchange with a close friend? Are you searching for answers that will help win an argument with a colleague? Maybe you're tired of years of conflict between family members? Or are you anxiously anticipating the upcoming holidays and desperately hoping for advice on how to survive the inevitable drama that results from talking politics? Regardless of your reasons, honesty is the best policy. The more truthful we can be with ourselves, the greater the prospect of our conversations being constructive.

Whenever we embark on any journey, it makes a big difference to understand ourselves before approaching the starting line. Many of us attempt to tackle ambitious goals—*I want to lose weight; I want to get that promotion; I want to be liked by others; I want to have a constructive conversation*—without first taking inventory. Because we really want to meet our goals and they are often challenging, it's not uncommon to hastily implement a solution before thinking it through or fully understanding how our unique characteristics and needs might impact the chosen solution.

For example, let's say your friend was able to lose ten pounds in four weeks after starting a 5:00 a.m. boot camp exercise class. You decide to do the same, without taking into account that the same approach may not work for you. While your friend is and has always been a morning person, you are and have always been a night owl. So, getting up at 4:30 a.m. to get to a 5:00 a.m. exercise class is doomed to fail before you even start. Let's be honest: if you're not naturally a chipper morning person, getting up at an ungodly hour so some drill sergeant can scream in your face is not going to be fun or sustainable. If you understand this about yourself, however, you might plan to first adjust your sleep schedule, or to find an evening class.

We've all been there. Our earnestness and even desperation can make us move too quickly and carelessly toward a solution. We want so badly to fix a problem or fulfill a goal that we don't slow down enough to figure out what we really want, why we want it, and what it will take for us to get the job done. Instead, we chase one diet fad after another, sign up for the latest exercise craze, and mindlessly follow and consume media recommendations for what we should always and never do. Are eggs good for you or not? What about coconut oil?

And then we feel confused, frustrated, and even hopeless when we don't get results, or they don't last, or aren't sustainable. In this vicious cycle of information overload, quick-fix promises, and inevitable failure, we lose connection with ourselves. We forget that the most important part of any solution, no matter what we are trying to achieve, is us. The better we know ourselves—what we like and dislike, what we need and don't need, how we operate, our strengths and limitations—the better our chances at success. The solution might be that 5:00 a.m. boot camp, but in order to make it work for you, you first need to have an honest conversation with yourself.

Having constructive conversations is no different. We know you are eager to get started. You may want to just skim the pages or stop partway through the book because you want to get there already! We get it—and we all know how well shortcuts work out in the end. Because we want you to succeed, we encourage you to be patient and take the time you need and deserve to make this work. So first things first, stand in front of that mirror. This initial—and arguably most important—constructive conversation will be with yourself. You are a big player in the journey ahead. You are also the person with whom you have the greatest influence.

So look in that mirror. Take an honest inventory. The work starts now.

Your Turn

Throughout this book, you will be invited to take a turn in your personal journal. By answering questions, writing down your ideas, and noting your self-reflections, you will play an active role throughout this process.

Let's get started. Take a few minutes to jot down the answers to the questions listed below. The first set of questions asks about your goals; the second set about your general personality characteristics; and the final set about your skills.

We invite you to be boldly honest. No filters. None of that scripted, rehearsed nonsense that you've been hiding behind for so long. Just the truth.

What's in It for You?

1. What or who motivated you to pick up this book?

2. Why are you reading it?

3. What or who are you trying to fix?

4. What do you believe is the real problem?

Read over your answers and see what you notice. Are your answers what you expected they would be? Are you surprised by any of your responses? Are you being truthful? The answers to these four questions should provide you with a good sense of where, why, and how you are starting off in this process.

Now let's turn to questions regarding your personality characteristics that might play a significant role in learning to have these important conversations.

The Good, the Bad, and the Ugly

1. In general, how do you manage disagreement or conflict? Do you approach it head-on? Or do you avoid it at all costs? Do you hope and pray it goes away by itself or is forgotten altogether? In your relationships, how are disagreements or conflicts usually resolved, if at all?

2. In general, how do you manage strong emotions? Are you the type of person who becomes easily agitated? Or does it take a lot to get you rattled? Do you shut down? Or do you move quickly to deescalate the strong emotion? Are certain emotions more challenging for you than others?

3. In general, what are your pet peeves about other people? How do you deal with these when they come up in conversations?

Again, read over your answers. Any observations? Surprises? Is the reflection in the mirror becoming clearer?

Now for the final set of questions. Knowing your personal style and skills at the start of this book can provide interesting and important insight as you embark on the constructive conversations endeavor. Ideally, it will give you some sense of where you are and in what ways you might want or need to grow.

What's Your Flow?

From "very poor" (0) to "excellent" (5), how would you rate your skills in the following areas?

1. Tolerating conflict

2. Managing disagreement in relationships

3. Regulating strong emotions, such as anger and fear

4. Self-reflection

5. Patience

6. Compassion for others

7. Self-compassion

The answers to the above questions should provide you with a baseline regarding your expectations for this book, your general personality disposition, and your skills level at the start of this journey. Your abilities in dealing with conflict, regulating emotions, self-reflection, patience, and compassion for yourself and others will be critical elements to having constructive conversations.

These conversations are not too different fundamentally from difficult conversations present in any relationship. However, conversations about culture and diversity are often loaded with social taboos and politically (in)correct landmines. This, in turn, makes them high-stakes for many people, as they risk possible misunderstandings, conflicts, and ruptures in their relationships. It is therefore not uncommon to find yourself avoiding such conversations altogether or jumping ship before it sinks.

Hot Topics

In the current volatile political climate, any conversation on culture and diversity is potentially loaded, if not explosive. It feels like there are virtually no safe or easy topics. As a result, there's a greater risk of getting sucked into the divisive vitriol—nasty. Twitter storms, political stalemates, and tit for tat—further fueling hatred and pain. Not surprisingly, this leads to higher blood pressure, as well as to greater distance and deeper divide between families, friends, and communities.

If you have been able to escape this pull, then you may be experiencing the other extreme: A total shutdown. Disengagement. Disconnection. Unfortunately, the initial impact of denial and delusion usually gives way to numbness and ultimately the same outcome as the first scenario—greater distance and deeper divide between families, friends, and communities.

All this just goes to show that undertaking the challenge of having constructive conversations, against such an intense backdrop, is not easy! In fact, it has made the stakes of taking risks to broach conversations on any cultural topic uncomfortably high. It has also made the stakes of *not* broaching such conversations even higher still.

It may feel like you either get sucked in all the way or you steer totally clear from any of these topics. However, we need to both stay engaged *and* not get hijacked by our feelings or others' reactions. Neither attacking nor retreating is the answer. We need to find middle ground. We need to move toward and soften into these uncomfortable spaces within ourselves and between one another.

Hopefully, we haven't amplified your anxiety too much about the risks and imperatives in having constructive conversations. Remember, we are in this together. Focus again on being bravely honest with yourself. In addition to the seemingly combustible nature of anything related to culture or diversity these days, we each have certain topics that are more sensitive or challenging than others. Maybe disability, gender equity, or environmental justice are particularly challenging for you. Or maybe you struggle most with conversations about class and material privilege. What topic is most challenging for you? By zeroing in on our own hot topics and blind spots, we become more capable of dealing with others—even when we disagree.

Anatasia's Turn

I am not proud to admit that on several occasions I have actually terminated relationships with people because of conversations on race that went awry. Without a doubt, I am most sensitive to topics on race, followed by class and gender.

Why? Because many of my most painful experiences have involved these aspects of my identity. If race and racism somehow enter a conversation, especially in a racially mixed setting, I usually find that I'm holding my breath, waiting for the mood in the room to shift, and bracing myself for the inevitable racist comment.

"I never thought of you as Asian, just a person, like me." "It's not fair that she got an interview and I didn't, just because I'm white." "Why do we always have to talk about race?" "If people don't like it here in America, they should just leave." "I bet he's going to pull the race card."

Depending on the nature and severity of the offensive comment, my relationship with the people involved, and whether I have enough energy at that particular moment to go there, the range of my responses in the past have included the following: pretended I didn't hear the comment and prayed it would not be revisited (avoidance, no energy to go there); clarified (or not) and then challenged what was said (confrontation, adequate energy level); or mentally recorded the racist comment and made a note to myself to never engage with that person again (avoidance, regardless of energy level I'm too hurt to even try to respond).

As you can see, my previous operating mode left much to be desired. It wasn't just the racist comments or behaviors. It was also me. I can be hotheaded, defensive, unforgiving, and stubborn. And when I am intensely hurt because of a highly offensive racist comment or because someone I trust said it, my habit had been to simply walk away. That deep pain, of a wounded soul, has often felt too great to tolerate, never mind actively manage in a potentially adversarial situation.

But walking away and ending relationships never lessened my pain or solved the problems that created it in the first place. It did the opposite. Thankfully, with age, training, and my own personal work, I have slowly disentangled myself from my old habits. I have learned to patiently and compassionately tend to my wounds and pain. And as I heal, I am better able to respond with understanding and compassion instead of reacting out of anger and fear.

That said, when it comes to race and racism, I find that I am still particularly vulnerable. So I continue to rely heavily on the Kim Constructive Conversations Model when engaging about race or racism. Whereas I only need a moment's notice to get going on most topics of culture and diversity, with race and racism, my heart still remains tender. I have to remind myself to be mindful and to take my time, to breathe, and to ground. It is in situations like these, where I am most sensitive, that I have found the 8 steps to be most helpful. When I am able to acknowledge this and be honest with myself, it can and has made a world of difference.

Your Turn

Go back to your journal and consider the following questions. As a guide, here are some topics on culture and diversity that you might reference (this is certainly not an exhaustive list): sexism, gender equality, immigration, racism, Black Lives Matter, Islamophobia, class, food insecurity, environmental justice, ableism, transphobia, reproductive rights, heterosexism, neurodiversity, and ageism.

1. What topic around culture and diversity is the *least* challenging for you? Why?

   - *When you consider having constructive conversations about this topic, what feelings come to mind? How do you relate to those emotions?*

2. What topic around culture and diversity is the *most* challenging? Why?

   - *When you consider having constructive conversations about this topic, what feelings come to mind? How do you relate to those emotions?*

Knowing where we stand at the start of a journey is crucially important. Remember, we are all our most valuable tools. As such, identifying and understanding the strengths and challenges that we are already carrying can be enormously helpful. When we do this at the beginning of our journey, we are less surprised and untethered by the inevitable appearance of these issues and emotions during our travels. This, in turn, will ensure we stay on course through the unavoidable ups and downs of the journey ahead.

Now let's get to those steps!

IDENTIFY A
GROUNDED GOAL

Identifying one's goals for constructive conversations is no simple task. Such conversations are not suited for all situations. Inherent in the definition of a constructive conversation is an understanding of and willingness for reciprocity—I will talk *and* I will also listen. This ultimately involves not only an exchange of words, but more important, an openness to deeply connect and ideally be mutually impacted.

Talking *at* someone, without any real intention to hear the other person's experience, does not qualify as a constructive conversation. Yes, we know this is tempting. You might even convince yourself that you need to put the other person in their place. To call them out for their racist, sexist, or classist microaggression—to educate them. Perhaps you feel that in fact you are offering an important public service, at no charge. You may have even had fantasies about how you might do this—or maybe you have done it.

But remember, such transient comments and critiques of others' behaviors, views, and experiences, no matter how satisfying they might be in the moment, are *not* constructive conversations. We admit that under certain circumstances, they might be appropriate or even necessary, but constructive and potentially healing exchanges they are not. In fact, they often cause more bad feelings and further compound relationship disconnections.

The task of identifying one's goal for constructive conversations requires much thought and reflection. In this first step of the Kim Constructive Conversations Model, you will learn to identify your personal goals through a process of self-inquiry, reflection, and grounding. You will also examine how strong emotions, self-healing, and unresolved history might impact those goals.

Identifying Your Goals: Round 1

This first round of identifying a goal will help you understand where you are starting from. As we mentioned in the introduction, how we get started is critically important and can play a big role in how the process ahead will unfold. This initial run is pretty straightforward—so let's get to it!

Your Turn

Turn to your journal and take a few minutes to write down your answers to the following questions.

1. What is your goal in learning how to have constructive conversations about culture and diversity?

2. With whom, in what context, and regarding what topic would you most like to have constructive conversations?

3. What specific outcome are you seeking?

Maybe your goal in learning how to have constructive conversations is to convince your sister that she was wrong in voting for a politician who has been accused of sexually harassing women. Maybe the specific outcome you are seeking is for your sister to realize she was wrong in how she voted and to ensure she votes for the "right" person next time. And maybe the result of having a successful constructive conversation would be a greater sense of ease with family members, and in particular with your sister. Maybe you believe this will ultimately help you feel less anxious and angry, and more hopeful.

Here are some other goals that might ring true for you:

- *I want to stand up for a marginalized group.*

- *I want to stand up for myself.*

- *I want to support someone I care about.*

- *I want to genuinely understand where someone is coming from.*

- *I want to share a different perspective, to help contribute to the discussion.*

- *I want to take a risk, to connect with someone with a different perspective, experience, or identity.*

If these hypothetical goals were your own, how do you think they would fare as constructive conversations?

Meet Tim and Rose: Constructive Conversations with Coworkers

Consider the following. Tim is a white man in his late twenties and is excited to be a part of a search committee at his work to recruit a new team member. One of the goals of his company is to increase staff diversity.

After multiple rounds of interviews, Tim recommends making the first offer to a Black applicant who meets qualifications for the position. His senior colleague Rose—a white woman who is also on the search committee—suggests hiring a white applicant who has commensurate qualifications with the Black applicant. Rose says that she feels it would be "reverse racism" if they do not select the white applicant.

Tim is confused, as he understood that one of the main goals of the search committee was to prioritize the hiring of qualified applicants who have been historically underrepresented in their company. Tim likes Rose and has a strong and friendly working relationship with her; in fact, it was Rose who recruited Tim for his current position. Thus, Tim is uncomfortable and hesitant about how to express his confusion and frustration to Rose. She's a senior employee who outranks him and is well regarded in their company. What would happen if Tim challenged her?

In Tim's case, maybe his goal would be to have an honest conversation with Rose about racial inequities in general and workplace diversity in particular. In spite of both having been tasked with helping to diversify the staff, it's clear that Tim and Rose have different feelings about the matter. These differences have led to unexpected tension and subsequently an uncomfortable stalemate between Tim and Rose. In broaching the subject, Tim might be hoping to convince Rose that the right candidate for the job is the Black applicant.

A secondary and related goal might be to reconnect with Rose, a colleague whom he respects, but whose actions on the search committee have left Tim both disappointed and uncertain about the future of their working relationship.

Do you think Tim will be able to meet his goals as he attempts a constructive conversation with Rose?

Hold on briefly while we veer slightly off course. We will soon come back to your goals and answers.

Grounding

In our fast-paced world and busy lives, we are vulnerable to disconnection from ourselves at any given moment. Of course we can't physically disconnect from our bodies, but daily stressors and responsibilities can pull us away from being present with our physical sensations, thoughts, and feelings. For example, many of us mindlessly eat beyond the point of satiation. We force our bodies to stay awake with cup after cup of caffeine, long past our bedtime. We often don't realize the stress we carry until we find ourselves battling road rage or yelling at our children. When we are pulled too far, we can become disconnected from our experiences entirely, making it harder to see things for what they are, and making it hard to know what we really need and desire.

Before setting your goal, it is important to have a clear mind space that will help you to identify what you truly want. We will call this process *grounding*.

It's essential that you pause before diving into something as important as constructive conversations. Often, there is such urgency, such a strong desire for immediate relief, that we act before we think. In fact, if you are like many people, various topics around culture and diversity can create in you a tornado of physical, cognitive, emotional, psychological, or even spiritual experiences. It can become a full-body affair.

Imagine for a moment the following scenario: You are at your partner's work holiday party and a stranger asks you about income inequality in the US and who you think is responsible—Republicans or Democrats? (We know, this conversation should come with a big bright warning sign that reads "Wrong Way! Turn Around!") For whatever reason, and against your better judgment (as well as your partner's plea to lay low), you decide to accept the invitation to dialogue, given how passionate you are about this particular topic.

Depending on a number of factors, the outcome of this scenario can range from wonderful to terrible. If you and the stranger share similar political views, you might feel connected and even begin to enjoy the party with your new friend. If, however, you share vastly different political ideologies, you might get into a heated debate, much to your partner's chagrin. Or you might retreat with a polite nod, once again reminded to avoid social landmines such as talking politics with strangers. In the latter case, you are likely activated, agitated, and ready to leave the party.

In spite of their challenging nature, many of us know that, fundamentally, conversations about difficult topics are not only important, but more and more they have become a moral mandate. We can't afford to not talk with one another; we must come together.

So what to do? How to respond and engage when every part of your body and mind are telling you, *Don't do it, there's no way out, nothing good ever comes of these discussions, it's social suicide.*

First and foremost, we ground. Before embarking on the important journey of constructive conversations, we must first pause, turn inward, and find our internal anchor. Grounding, especially in the presence of strong emotions, is critical and can prove powerfully effective.

How Do I Ground?

There are many ways to ground. Central to any grounding, however, is the practice of mindful awareness, or simply mindfulness: to slow down and be present. In spite of how simple this may sound, mindfulness requires some effort and practice. This is because we are creatures of habit, and many of us have become caught up in the fast-paced world around us.

As a global community, we are constantly plugged in. We are consistently bombarded with endless to-do lists, deadlines, and responsibilities, as well as cultural demands to do more and be better in all aspects of our lives. The powerful influence of social media demands constant striving, grasping, attaching, and artificially connecting. The outcome of all this is that we are frequently disconnected from our bodies, thoughts, feelings, and experiences. Instead, we function on automatic pilot. Unaware. Mindless. Slowing down and grounding can feel unfamiliar and even challenging at first.

In recent decades, the practice of mindfulness has gradually spread throughout the Western mainstream, both culturally and as a field of science. Its positive effects on various aspects of life have been evidenced broadly, including in the field of mental health. In fact, the third wave of cognitive behavioral therapy models has been dominated by the practice of mindfulness and related ideas from Eastern philosophy in general and Buddhism in particular.

Our inclusion of mindfulness is not intended to promote any particular religious doctrine. The popularity and effects of this powerful practice are undeniable, and it can become an invaluable tool for constructive conversations. If nothing else, we should find some comfort in the fact that these teachings have been around for thousands of years!

Here are some suggestions for how you might experience grounding. We encourage you to try a few of these and see which have traction for you. Commit to doing it daily. What do you have to lose? Don't be afraid to explore and experiment. Have fun with it!

Grounding the body:

- Meditation

- Diaphragmatic (deep abdominal) breathing

- Mindful movement such as yoga, dance, or hiking

- Mindful sensing of a loving hug, warm bath, or gentle massage

Grounding the mind:

- Inhale "calm" and exhale "stress."

- Chant personal mantra (e.g., "I can do this." "I believe and trust in myself").

- Gently challenge irrational thoughts (e.g., *Is it really true that I will never get better, no matter what I do? Is it accurate to say I always fail at this. What do I mean by "fail"?*).

- Become curious about strong emotions instead of succumbing to them (e.g., *Where is all this agitation coming from? What am I afraid of?*).

Your Turn

Turn again to your journal and write down your answers to the following questions.

1. What person, place, thing, activity, and mind-set best allow me to slow down?

2. What is required in order for me to become fully aware of my body and breath?

3. What is required in order for me to become fully aware of my thoughts and feelings, without judgment or attachment?

4. In the past, when I wanted or needed to calm down, what helped?

5. My best personal tools for grounding and becoming aware and mindful are…

Now pick any of the grounding tools you just identified and try it out. Maybe it's closing your eyes and taking ten deep breaths or making yourself a cup of your favorite tea and mindfully savoring every sip. Whatever it is, take a break from reading and do it now.

…

Welcome back. Following your mindfulness practice, ask yourself the following questions. Write down your answers in your journal.

1. How does your body feel? Do you feel less anxious or more grounded?

2. What thoughts and feelings came up during this exercise?

3. Are you generally aware of what you are thinking, feeling, and sensing?

4. How connected are you to your thoughts, feelings, and senses when it comes to topics of culture and diversity?

5. Are there certain topics that bring you greater or less sense of ease? Why? What is your personal connection to or experience with these topics?

How Grounding Helps

Grounding through mindfulness doesn't necessarily mean changing your initial goals. Rather, it provides us the opportunity to examine *why* we have chosen the goals that we have. This in turn enriches the meaning and substance of those goals. It gives us a chance to reflect and to connect at a deeper level with our intentions.

For example, grounding through mindfulness does not mean we should not be angry. Instead, it becomes a means through which we begin to understand *why* we are angry. Maybe you have personally been impacted by economic injustice. Maybe the experience of growing up in poverty is still very raw and painful for you and your family. As such, maybe your goal in conversing with the stranger at the holiday party is ultimately not about asking him, "What's the matter with you?!" for supporting the "wrong" political party. Rather, beneath the surface of outrage and anger, maybe it's really about a wish for another person to see, believe, and be impacted by the truth of your painful experience. Maybe even for someone "across the aisle" to understand and validate that, even though your anger might be hard to tolerate, your pain is justified. When we ground, the truth of what we are ultimately seeking comes into greater clarity.

Mindfulness practices, such as the ones you identified in your journal, are excellent ways to ground anytime, anywhere. If you can turn this into a regular practice, it will be a tremendous help when you need it most.

Now that we have grounded, let's return to your goals from the first part of this step.

Identifying Your Goals: Round 2

If we don't know *where* we are going, or *why* we are going there, it's hard to know how or in which direction to travel. Now that you are grounded and feel more connected to yourself, let's turn back to the goals you identified just a few pages ago. Revisit the same questions and also consider the follow-up inquiries.

In this second round, instead of focusing solely on the content aspects of your answers, invite a fuller level of awareness and connection. This will allow you to fine-tune and deepen goals that reflect the greater truth of your intentions.

Your Turn

Write down your answers to the following questions in your journal.

1. What is your goal in learning how to have constructive conversations about culture and diversity? *Why is this*

personally important to you? What would it mean to you to have constructive conversations?

2. With whom, in what contexts, and regarding what topics would you most like to have constructive conversations? *Why this particular person, context, or topic? Have you had any significant personal experience with this person, context, or topic? What would it mean to you to have constructive conversation with this person, in this context, or on this topic?*

3. What specific outcome are you seeking? *Why? What would it mean to you personally if this outcome was realized?*

Recall the vignette above regarding the two sisters. The goal in the first round—trying to convince your sister that she was wrong in voting for a politician accused of sexual harassment—was based almost entirely on your impulses and emotional reactions. After taking time to ground, you are able to reflect and realize that like so many women, you have experienced a lifetime of sexual harassment. So too has your sister. Though you and your sister have not always seen eye to eye, you generally assume that the two of you share similar life values. So her decision to vote for someone you vehemently oppose came as a shock. If you did have a constructive conversation with your sister on this matter, it would mean a chance to share with her *why* you felt so betrayed and pained by her political decision. It might mean you don't have to distance yourself from her in spite of your initial impulse to lash out or turn away. It might also mean an opportunity for deeper understanding so that when the next vote is cast, you and your sister can connect from a place of mutual respect, support, and hope.

Grounding allows us again and again to anchor in our true intentions and experiences. Our initial reactions to challenging situations often activate impulses, which we might later regret or which ultimately do not serve us. In the case of Tim and Rose, it might feel great in the moment for Tim to turn to Rose and exclaim, "What is wrong with you?!" That would certainly communicate Tim's outrage and disapproval of Rose's decision. However, this reaction would most likely not lead to a constructive conversation. In fact, reactive responding is the opposite of a constructive conversation. Inherent in the latter is an openness for meaningful dialogue and connection, not an impulsive reprimand, no matter how justified you might be. So, if your intention in having constructive conversations is to correct, criticize, shame, and reprimand, you are reading the wrong book. Instead, if you seek deeper understanding and opportunities to work and heal together, keep reading—you are on the right track.

Pause here once again. Go back to your grounding. Have your original goals shifted in any way? Maybe in content or essence? Ideally, the review of your goals after grounding will allow you to identify a greater sense of understanding, meaning, and connectedness to *why* you are really reading this book.

Strong Emotions

First, it goes without saying that central to constructive conversations is the presence of strong emotions: anger, fear, outrage, anxiety, sadness, frustration, urgency, and hope. Thankfully our strong emotions can give us clues to our most legitimate goals. When we locate our feelings, it's important to pause and observe them with curiosity. *Why am I feeling so angry? What am I so anxious about? What am I afraid of?* Frequently, strong emotions take over to set an agenda without the consent of our rational minds, thereby sabotaging our goals. To make matters worse, if those strong emotions are negative in nature, they can hide the more vulnerable and important feelings buried beneath—the feelings that ultimately lead us to what we are seeking and needing.

Not all emotions are created equal. Some help facilitate connections with other people, while others impede them. Emotions psychotherapists often refer to as "secondary," such as anger, can hinder healthy ways of relating and communicating. This is especially true if they get in the way of awareness about related "primary" emotions. Secondary, or surface-level emotions, often obfuscate the more vulnerable primary emotions beneath the surface, such as pain and fear.

Maybe it hurts you deeply to consider the possibility that your own sister might not champion the plight of women? That she might ultimately not support you? These kinds of insights position your goals for constructive conversations from a qualitatively different place than if you were operating only with the secondary emotion of anger. If we can identify and become curious about our surface-level emotions (e.g., anger, agitation, anxiety, depression), they will invariably lead us to our deeper emotions. Those deeper, more vulnerable emotions (especially pain and fear) in turn will allow us to explore and unpack the *why* question and ultimately better situate ourselves for the emergence of our most genuine constructive conversation goals.

Your Turn

Take a few minutes to locate any strong emotions as you again review your goals. Write down your answers to the following questions in your journal.

Regarding your goals:

1. Can you identify any related primary (deeper) emotions such as pain and fear?

2. What or who brings you pain?

3. What are you afraid of?

4. How might these deeper emotions give you clues about your most honest intentions for constructive conversations?

Challenging Ourselves to Dig Deep

Another variable to consider in identifying your goal is the often misguided assumption that constructive conversations are mostly about someone or something other than ourselves.

In spite of what may be our initial goal—to change the mind and perspective of another person—much of this work is about us and our own healing. Healing in relationship connection is important, given that so much of our suffering is related to or generated in the context of relationships. Maybe part of your anxiety about having a constructive conversation with your queer Guatemalan coworker stems from your guilt about your white and heterosexual privilege. Maybe you have had negative experiences in previous attempts to connect with people of color and LGBT folks. Maybe you are afraid you will mess it up again or that your emotional overwhelm will once more get in the way. The opposite could also be true. Maybe you are the queer Guatemalan coworker anxious about broaching a constructive conversation with your straight white colleague. This may be the result of negative past experiences, your outrage about others' inability or unwillingness to acknowledge their privilege, or even your own internalized racism and heterosexism. As is evident, our true experiences are often exponentially more complex and nuanced than we realize.

Our task then is not only to identify our strong emotions, but as well to understand from where they have come and how they operate to obscure our deeper experiences and intentions. Such insight will prove invaluable to how we relate to ourselves and ultimately to one another.

In many ways, the practice of constructive conversations is about the opportunity to uncover and speak our personal truths. As such, we need to dig deep. If we don't recognize and connect to our real experiences, in spite of our good intentions, it will only be a matter of time before our impulsive emotional reactions escape and take over. This means we have to start by articulating goals that bravely and clearly speak the truth of our experiences. Only in this way do we protect ourselves from unintended, unhelpful, and often unkind reactions running the show.

Your Turn

Write down your answers to the following questions in your journal.

1. When do you feel angry, pained, or afraid regarding matters of culture and diversity?

2. What are your personal experiences in these areas?

3. What healing, if any, is needed for you?

4. How will being in connection with another person through constructive conversations facilitate your healing?

The Unresolved Trauma of Our Collective Past

A final variable for consideration in identifying your goal is recognizing the unresolved trauma of our collective past. The intergenerational transmission of historical trauma in the form of imperialism, genocide, slavery, apartheid, internment, systematic marginalization, and oppression is not easily forgotten or erased. Indeed, the residuals of our past continue to dictate and fuel present-day cultural divides, social inequities, and relationship ruptures for all of us.

Much like a family with a long history of baggage, we are a people systematically disconnected, deluded, separated, and paralyzed by a past that continues to profoundly influence our experiences with ourselves and one another. This heavy burden makes the seemingly simple task of having a conversation humbly challenging. Acknowledging and even opening Pandora's box is no small matter.

Let's go back once more to the two sisters. What might be the contextual variables at play? In spite of the liberation and rights gained during the women's movement decades ago, female-identified persons have and continue to be denigrated and marginalized in many spheres of contemporary society. For example, women are severely underrepresented in most positions of power, including in government and other leadership roles. Female-identified persons are also disproportionately victims of sexual abuse, assault, exploitation, and violence.

Against this backdrop, the singular incident of your sister's vote for the politician accused of sexual harassment is understood as a much greater issue than the bad feelings between the two of you. Institutionalized gender oppression and culturally sanctioned sexism are dynamics and realities that have been inherited across generations. As such, the pain related to these topics is often as deep as their roots. Understanding this—that the matter is so much greater than the singular incident before you—can provide an important frame of reference and embolden your commitment to healing through constructive conversations.

It is both personal and not personal. It is about you and your sister. And it is about so much more. It's about your anger and fear that your sister might not support you and other female-identified persons. It's also about the long and difficult history of sexism and internalized sexism that has been and continues to insidiously thrive in the broader culture. So, your initial goal of getting your sister to realize how "wrong" she was and how she can cast the "right" vote in the future can now be viewed with further levels of depth, complexity, and meaning. You might still have these goals, but understanding *why* you feel so strongly and *how* they are connected to a greater context can allow you to move more easily through and beyond the unhelpful emotional reactions. Awaiting you on the other end of this self-exploration is even greater clarity, grounding, and resolve toward your values—as well as compassion for yourself and your loved ones, even when you don't see eye to eye.

Summary

So the takeaway from Step 1 is this: identifying your goal for constructive conversations involves a number of considerations. First, before doing anything else, ground yourself by turning inward. Use your own unique grounding tools to practice mindfulness of body, thoughts, and feelings.

Once you are grounded, clearly articulate your goal for wanting to have a constructive conversation. Simultaneously consider the presence of any strong emotions. Are they connected in any way to more vulnerable, deeper emotions that can provide clues about your true intentions? What about the role of your own healing? In some way, is part of your goal about calming your fear or healing your pain? Remember, understanding *why* you wish to have a constructive conversation, including why you might be angry, afraid, or hurting, is critically important to developing a viable goal. Without understanding, you cannot neutralize or manage your strong emotions.

Finally, step away just a bit from your personal attachment to all of this, and create room for the gravity and magnitude of the issues involved. Hopefully, reminding yourself of how pervasive and long-standing these challenges are gives you some sense of context and perspective, as well as an invitation for patience and compassion.

Finalize your goals. Jot down some related notes. We are now ready for Step 2.

LOCATE AND ACKNOWLEDGE BARRIERS

Now that you know what your goal is, it is time to anticipate what challenges might arise when working toward this goal. To do this, you will examine your blind spots, and take inventory of the internal and external barriers that will likely come up.

We will first consider the internal barriers, because we usually have the most power to change these. After all, they only involve one person, ourselves. We will then examine any external barriers, which typically involve other people or larger systems. By being real with yourself about the expected roadblocks, when they do pop up you will not be surprised or become paralyzed by them. Instead, you will be prepared and ready to create a plan to decrease the barriers or work right through them. If you skip this step, the barriers will likely win and the conversation will not happen, at least not the one you intended. By thinking through a complete list of barriers, you will significantly increase your chances of success for engaging in the full constructive conversation process.

Know Thyself: Where Are Your Blind Spots?

How do we know what our individual barriers might be? The reflection and self-assessment you completed in Step 1 will help you immensely with this step. Lean in with gentle curiosity to find out more about what personal hurdles might be in the way of accomplishing your goal. Be real with yourself about your subjectivity, blind spots, and even your deficits.

The Johari window, created by psychologists Joseph Luft and Harrington Ingham (1955), visually demonstrates four ways people understand themselves in relation to their own and others' view. There are four windows or "selves": known, hidden, blind, and unknown. The known window consists of things both we and others know about ourselves. The hidden window, or private self, includes the private things we know about ourselves, but that others don't know. The blind window contains aspects that others see, but that we ourselves are unaware of. The unknown self is the unconscious part of us that neither ourselves nor others know about.

1 **Known Self** Things we know about ourselves and others know about us	**2** **Hidden Self** Things we know about ourselves that others do not know
3 **Blind Self** Things others know about us that we do not know	**4** **Unknown Self** Things neither we nor others know about us

Using the Johari framework, to know yourself means to increase the size of the open window as well as the hidden self, by decreasing both the blind spot and unknown squares. By doing this, your knowledge of yourself grows.

Your Turn

Turn to your journal to answer questions that will help you think about your personalized Johari window, or four aspects of yourself.

Known Self

- *How well do I know myself?*

- *What experiences, activities, and life events have really helped me get to know myself? How would I describe myself to someone I just met?*

- *How have others described me?*

- *What have others told me are my biggest strengths and areas for growth?*

- *How do I come across to people when I speak to them? How does this vary depending on the person? How about the setting? Or other circumstances, such as when I'm rushed, tired, or late?*

Hidden Self

- *What important things do others not know about me?*

- *What is helpful about others not knowing these things?*

- *What's unhelpful about these things being hidden?*

- *Would I want any of these things to move to the known self?*

- *If so, which ones? If not, why not?*

Blind Self

- *Who knows me better than I know myself?*

- *What would that person say to me if I told them about my constructive conversation goals?*

- *What might they advise me about my goals?*

- *Who do I trust that also tends to see the world very differently from the way I do? If asked, what might that person say about my personality, my strengths, and my areas for growth?*

Unknown Self

- *How do I feel about the idea of an unconscious?*

- *What might possibly be unknown about myself?*

- *How could I go about accessing this unknown information?*

By answering the above questions, you have made progress toward increasing the known self, and lessening the blind and unknown self.

Now let's turn to another activity that can help you learn more about your blind spots. In this day and age of smart technology, it's time to put it to good use.

Using your phone, computer, or some type of recording device, take a video of yourself, pretending to talk to someone about one of your goals for a constructive conversation. No, you don't have all the steps yet, but the point is to notice how you naturally talk about your goal. Time yourself talking for 1–2 minutes. Then play it back.

How does your voice sound? What are your go-to words? What facial expressions do you have? What is your eye contact like? Watching yourself in this way will help increase your awareness about your verbal and nonverbal communication style.

Now think of someone you trust and ask them to watch this video too. Ask them to tell you their impressions of what you said and how you said it—as honestly as possible. See if some of your blind self can come in through the open window.

Alicia's Turn

I have received many gifts from family, friends, and colleagues that helped to make my known self larger. For example, I didn't realize how much I used my hands to speak until a colleague of mine took photos of me during a presentation I was giving. Also, my mom informed me that I say "actually" and "good point" frequently when expressing myself. And my husband often puts up a mirror to my tendency to overexplain things and my difficulty getting to the point.

Each and every time I learn something new about how I express myself and how I come across to others, I'm both surprised and intrigued. *How did I not know this already?* But I didn't. Being open to realizing and learning new things about myself is crucial to understanding how I impact others.

What Barriers Are Standing in Your Way?

Close your eyes for a second and imagine the barriers that are preventing you from engaging in a difficult dialogue. What boulders are in your way? Experienced hikers anticipate the terrain and come prepared for obstacles, such as unsteady ground and changes in climate and altitude. In turn, we ask you, our adventurous readers, about the barriers that may hinder or slow down your journey.

Ask yourself, *Is there anything about the goal I identified that is personally difficult for me?* Maybe the topic at hand is very important to your identity? Maybe it activates your own unresolved pain of being stigmatized? Questions like these will help guide you in identifying what internal barriers could stand in your way.

Internal Barriers

Internal barriers can take many forms, including personalized thoughts, behaviors, and feelings that stop us from pursuing our chosen goals. Regardless of the specific internal barriers you face, it is crucial that you identify them. If you fail to do so, the barriers will win and your constructive conversation will cease to happen.

Thoughts, such as negative self-statements, act as internal barriers when they discourage action and put us down. Examples might include, *You've never been good at talking to people, why start now?* Or

I don't know what I'm taking about, so I should just keep quiet. Or *My boss will never listen to what I have to say because I'm not as smart as he is.* These critical, discouraging thoughts need to be replaced with more hopeful, encouraging ones. For example, *I can do this, I am capable,* or *I'm willing to try.*

Behaviors can also block our goals. Perfectionism, procrastination, and avoidance are at the top of this list! As an example, when we don't know exactly what the right thing to say is in a difficult or uncomfortable situation, many of us say nothing. The moment passes, and we never get around to saying anything at all. Who are we kidding—we may even actively avoid that person so we don't have to engage with them at all! It is not easy to know what the "right" thing to do is, and it's very easy to become overwhelmed and thus do nothing. Our instinct to avoid something potentially negative is understandable and even rational. After all, who would deliberately make themselves vulnerable to stressful situations?

Your Turn

Pull out your journal and write down the answers to the following questions.

1. What negative thoughts interfere with you pursuing your goals? These thoughts may be about yourself, others, the world, and even the future. List them all, and then write down alternative positive statements to tell yourself instead.

2. What behaviors of yours get in the way of you reaching your goals? What roles do perfectionism, procrastination, and avoidance play in your life?

Fear

In presenting and teaching about constructive conversations at length, we have found that there is one emotion that seems to be the quintessential emotional barrier: fear. Fear of conflict, fear of losing control, fear of putting your foot in your mouth, fear of looking racist, fear of being judged, fear of being rejected, fear of being abandoned, fear of being vulnerable, fear of not being believed, or even fear of using your own power. All these fears can be fundamental barriers to pursuing constructive conversations about culture and diversity.

Some fear is evolutionarily adaptive and keeps us on guard and alert for real threats. And in some cases, there are real threats involved with fear: fear of retaliation; violence; loss of home, job, and safety; and in some instances fear of death. Unfortunately, for those among us who are the most marginalized and oppressed, these fears are all too real and must be taken seriously. For others, their fears, though not life-threatening, can still stand in their way of constructive conversations. Such fear perpetuates the status quo, by leading us to avoid real dialogue around important societal issues that need our shared attention.

It behooves us all to be reminded that there are those who face grave and persistent threats to their livelihood and safety. In spite of this, they speak up and courageously work toward liberation from injustice and toward our collective healing. Even though our own fears are not inconsequential, remembering this can bring us more courage to face them.

CASE STUDY

Consider a cisgender woman whom we will call Elaine. Elaine has identified the goal of talking to Robert and Lilly, her boyfriend's parents, about their transphobic assumptions and language. Elaine really likes her boyfriend's parents overall and envisions a future with her boyfriend, Alex. However, Elaine has been shocked, disturbed, and hurt upon hearing Lilly and Robert talk about their discomfort with all-gender restrooms, their mistrust of trans people in the military, and their occasional joke about transgender people's "confusion" about their identity. Elaine has a trans-identified brother, and so feels passionately about defending her brother; she also thinks ahead about what will happen if her brother and Alex's parents meet.

So far, whenever these incidents have arisen, Elaine has stayed quiet in the moment and vented only to Alex, later. Upon reflection, she noticed that while being quiet, she is feeling some intense emotions. If Elaine does not speak up, she fears that she is betraying her brother. She is afraid that her silence will communicate that she is ashamed of her brother and the trans community she cares about. She also feels angry and fearful that if she speaks up, she will erupt and not be able to control her criticism of her boyfriend's parents. Elaine is further afraid that by disagreeing with her boyfriend's parents, they may dislike her and no longer welcome her to family events. Elaine was also taught by her own parents to respect elders, and so she is additionally worried about violating this norm.

One of the overarching themes in Elaine's situation is, indeed, fear. Fear underlies the thoughts and concerns that have been keeping Elaine paused at best and paralyzed at worst. Elaine's dilemma initially appears dichotomous: to keep quiet or to speak out. But Elaine also has the option of engaging in a constructive conversation with Lilly and Robert. Her fear is the central barrier preventing that from happening.

If Elaine is able to be honest with herself about her fear, she can then troubleshoot it. Letting Alex know that she is considering this conversation will allow him to be a supportive presence for herself, as well as his parents—perhaps this could be one way to decrease the fear? Or Elaine may decide to journal about her fears, to give them the full space they need, before speaking in person with Lilly and Robert. Elaine can also role-play the worst-case scenario with Alex or someone else she trusts, and identify comforting words of wisdom she can use to help soothe her fears. Another idea might be to speak with only one parent at a time. As Elaine's fears are unpacked and given the care and consideration they need and deserve, more viable options for conversing will become available.

TURNING TOWARD OUR FEARS

So ask yourself, *What am I most afraid of? Do I get anxious and afraid just thinking about the prospect of having a constructive conversation?* If so, you are definitely not alone. The "why," however, is where our own unique histories and personalities come into play, as well as the unique circumstances of the situation at hand. Maybe you're worried about personal consequences such as loss of job, jeopardizing a promotion, or even losing an important relationship. Be proud for being open with yourself about your fear.

If you think you may be unclear about the true nature of your fears, try going back to the Johari window of the blind self. Consider reaching out to those who know you best and invite them to help you identify what your fears might be. Knowing our fears is crucial to facing them.

It's easy to become hijacked by anxiety, since engaging in constructive conversations means we are choosing to turn toward, not away, from our fears. Other common feelings that can contribute to us staying stagnant and mute are hopelessness, anger, and discomfort with uncertainty. A hopeless perspective creates doubt: *What's the point of having this conversation since nothing will change?* Anger can block new ideas from flowing and instead lead us to lash out. Our minds and bodies are conditioned to reject discomfort and pain, so it's no wonder that strong emotions can easily take us hostage under these circumstances. When the outcomes are uncertain, our very concept of self can feel threatened. To speak to others in a new way invites new possibilities, but many people don't like change. You may worry, *Am I abandoning who I used to be by acting or speaking in a new way?* You may fear, *My relationship with this person might change. Will they be mad at me? Will they look at me differently? Will they stop talking to me?*

Being prepared is an adaptive skill, and there's also a point where you need to trust in yourself and the process. Be open to change. If we remain committed only to a specific outcome, it will be very difficult to initiate and maintain constructive conversations. Finally, find inspiration from those around you, past and present, who bravely and boldly confronted their fears in spite of dire threats and consequences. You can do it too!

Your Turn

Time to face your fears. What are you afraid of? It's time to start chipping away at those fears. You don't have to wait for a constructive conversation to practice tackling your fears. Here are some suggestions for getting started right away. The better you can learn to confront and conquer your fears in these everyday situations, the more prepared you will be when it's time to have that constructive conversation.

Pull out your journal, and ponder the following questions.

1. Identify something that makes you anxious or afraid in your everyday life. Maybe saying hello to that person in class or at work that you'd like to get to know? Nervous to ask for help at the shopping mall? Terrified to try that new roller coaster ride?

2. Make a plan to conquer that fear, and follow through with your plan. Breaking up the feared activity into smaller parts and being specific with your planning will help you effectively chip away at your fear. Bring in your accountability buddy, if you have one, to help brainstorm ways to make this doable.

The more experience we have facing our fears, no matter how small, the more confident we become in taking on even more of them.

Defensiveness

Defensiveness is the enemy of good listening. The quickest way for a tough conversation to veer off course is by misperceiving the thoughts, feelings, and behaviors of the person you are talking to and then reacting in a knee-jerk way.

When someone says something that offends us, the initial purpose of the conversation can get hijacked. Then, instead of listening and being present in the moment, we start focusing on what we want to say next. We plan out what we will declare, once the other person stops talking, in order to defend our honor or explain ourselves. In the worst cases, when defensiveness has really derailed communication, we don't even wait for the other person to finish. Rather, we interrupt them and assert our own claims and truths. We often feel a relief of pressure in the moment, at being able to speak our mind, but later we may be left feeling dissatisfied, regretful, and further away from the goal of communicating.

Another common form of defensiveness is shutting down and leaving a conversation. If we are able to realize we are being defensive, we can prevent this internal barrier from taking over. For example, a commitment to openness at the outset can help curb our tendency to be defensive. In our previous example, because Elaine cares so much about her brother, she may understandably feel protective and guarded. But if she's preoccupied with only these feelings, she won't be able to really dialogue with her boyfriend's parents.

You may even become defensive while reading this book. This is understandable. If this happens, ask yourself, *What is so triggering for me?* If you are white or identify strongly with another privileged identity (such as wealthy, able-bodied, or male), a common reaction when thinking about social injustice is guilt. If you feel guilty, use it as a motivator to stay in the conversation—not a reason to excuse yourself from it. Don't let the defensiveness take over. Instead, stay curious and engaged. Of course, you can always decide to stop reading, but remember, you picked up this book for a reason. Get back in touch with those reasons.

Fatigue

Daily life keeps us busy in and of itself. Finding the extra energy to engage in constructive conversations can feel impossible when you are exhausted. You may have the will to converse, but lack the stamina to carry it out. When you are depleted, with nothing much to give to yourself or others, the last thing you want to do is talk about highly sensitive matters like racism, sexism, ableism, or any other ism! When you are on the downside of power, this may be especially true—because it takes an extra toll on us to confront issues with people who have more power and privilege than we do.

While you may occasionally decide to push through the fatigue, we think this is one of the barriers that is best addressed by slowing down. Instead of pushing forward with a constructive conversation, when the fatigue is too much, do some self-care. You can come back to the conversation later. Take that nap. Nourish your body with whatever it is you're missing. Go into your self-care tool kit, and get yourself back to an energy level where discussing tough topics is doable.

Your Turn

Do the exercises below to help you navigate your internal barriers through visual imagery and practicing good self-care.

Magic Bag Exercise

In the iconic movie *Mary Poppins,* Mary has a magic carpetbag from which she pulls many items that don't look like they could possibly fit in the bag: a tall plant, a coat hanger, a lamp. Whatever she needs at that moment, the bag is able to deliver.

We'd like you to imagine carrying around your own magic bag, filled with whatever you need in the moment to help you with the internal barriers you come up against. What will you fill your bag with? Here are some suggestions to get you started.

- *Kind words*

- *Inspirational quotes*

- *Lyrics of uplifting songs*

- *Pictures of your heroes and heroines*

- *Anything else that will help you navigate your internal barriers*

Use your imagination, and get creative. Maybe you will pack a whole bathtub for that long overdue bubble bath. Or maybe you'll pack a bottle-of-courage candy—just pick your favorite flavor and you're not afraid anymore. Remember, this bag is magical, so the sky's the limit!

Now, turn to your journal and draw your bag and its contents. If you're not an artist, that's okay! Remember, face your fears and be willing to try something even if it takes you out of your comfort zone.

Self-Care Jar Exercise

On small pieces of paper write down fifty ways you can take care of yourself. Here are some examples.

- *Go for a walk or run outside.*

- *Close your eyes and take ten deep breaths.*

- *Jump on a trampoline.*

- *Play your favorite sport.*

- *Go for a hike.*

- *Buy yourself some flowers.*

- *Read your favorite book.*

- *Soak your feet in hot water.*

- *Listen to your favorite song (preferably a relaxing or empowering one).*

- *Dance like no one is watching!*

- *Learn a new yoga pose.*

- *Treat yourself to a nice meal.*

- *Give yourself three compliments.*

- *Practice mindfulness in the shower.*

Fifty self-care activities might sound like a lot, but the idea is to come up with so many that when you go to the jar, you will always have a small but impactful deed to help nourish you.

If you get stuck, get other people involved. Ask people in your life, including your accountability buddy, what they do for self-care.

Fold the pieces of paper in half and place them in a mason jar (with the lid on, to protect these valuable ideas). Put the jar in a visible place, perhaps your kitchen table or the desk in your office. Go to the jar often to practice ways to nourish your body, mind, and spirit.

Common External Barriers

Beyond the parameters of our own minds, thoughts, and feelings, barriers also exist in the outside world. First and foremost, the larger context we all live in sets up these seemingly invisible walls of what we can and cannot talk about. Some topics, such as politics and religion, are considered off-limits at many people's dinner tables. We live in an era of blatant and subtle contradictions—political correctness and free speech, absolute truth and relativity, and permeable and impenetrable boundaries. With this as our backdrop, we can feel honest dialogue being silenced, discouraged, or at minimum already shaped and influenced before it even begins.

Social Norms

Like Elaine, many of us have been socialized to avoid hot topics that will lead to conflict or disagreement. We may feel we are violating social or familial norms by pursuing our goal in Step 1 because of the systems that tell us we should not have those kinds of conversations. Knowing that open conversations may fly in the face of this larger backdrop of macrosystems that encourage one to "keep the peace," "don't make waves," and "don't challenge the status quo," will hopefully be helpful to you.

Helpful how, you may ask? By reminding you that you are not making these things up. It can feel hard to initiate—because it *is* hard. In some ways, you are going against the grain. Don't get us wrong, the purpose of constructive conversations is not to "burn down the house." However, others may feel this is the case when you approach them, if only because this kind of compassionate communication happens so rarely.

Criticism and arguments, sometimes with name-calling and accusations, do occur when people attempt to broach issues of culture and diversity with people they disagree with.

Some of the most polarizing topics involve religion. An extreme example of this is the pro-life/pro-choice dichotomy. Those who take a pro-life stance have accused pro-choice believers of being murderers, and those who are pro-choice have accused the pro-life perspective of being anti-women. And then of course there's politics. A colleague of ours shared how her adult children are not speaking to her because of political differences sparked by Donald Trump winning the United States presidency. In a postelection survey cited by *The Wall Street Journal,* 31 percent of people in the U.S. reported having a "heated argument" with a friend or family member who voted differently from them (Eckel, 2017). The Pew Research Center also reported that after the 2016 presidential election, 59 percent of those in the US avoided talking about politics if all or most of their family members had a different political leaning. It's just a fact: people avoid conversations that they believe will lead to conflict.

However, with the 8-step approach, we have experienced and observed that it is possible to have these constructive conversations. Honest and sincere dialogue about such issues can actually lead to great intimacy between the people involved. Intimacy does not necessarily mean agreement. Rather, the conversation can make space for increased closeness and mutual understanding, which can hopefully lead to movement, mending, and even change.

Recipient's Story

The person on the receiving end of your talk can strongly influence how the conversation will go. More specifically, the personality of the recipient, the role the recipient has in your life, the history you share with the recipient, and other factors unique to this person all influence the trajectory of the dialogue. They may possess attributes, mannerisms, a communication style, or a kind of power over you that strongly impacts how you approach them, how you typically react to them, and which *internal* barriers you experience knowing you are initiating a constructive conversation with them. The external barriers are very important to identify as possible things that can get in the way of reaching one's goals.

It is also quite possible that the person you want to speak with simply does not care about the topic you are trying to broach. Apathy on the part of the other person can act as a big barrier to a constructive conversation. If someone is uninterested or indifferent to the conversation, this can stall progress. How frustrating! How can others not care at all about something you care so deeply about? It does take two to have a conversation, and if the other person is not a willing participant, you may be at a standstill.

Power, Privilege, and Marginalization

Who you are talking to matters, especially when it comes to the power dynamics between you and the other person. In any given situation, you might have more or less power, depending on factors such as age, gender, race, nationality, ethnicity, religion, and ability. If you are coming from a subjugated position and on the suppressed side of the power differential, it can be especially hard to speak your truth. This is one reason why people of color can easily become exhausted bringing up their experiences around discrimination, inequity, and cultural insensitivity in their schools and places of work. We have heard time and time again from our students, colleagues, friends, and clients of color that they feel the pressure of being a spokesperson on these issues in white spaces, and that this takes a toll on their health and well-being. In the case of Elaine, she identifies as female and is also younger than her boyfriend's parents. It can be extra challenging to be assertive and have constructive conversations with adults older than us, who we are often taught to think of as authority figures, as well as with men or father figures. Power is inherent in hierarchies. So, if you are a boss or employer broaching a conversation, know that this is also a possible barrier to a pending constructive conversation.

This can all get complicated very quickly. Let's say an Asian woman supervises a white man with a physical disability. Both people in this pair have power over the other in some way. There is no easy answer in these cases with complex intersecting identities. Instead of searching for a rigid formula to apply unilaterally across every situation and person, commit to being aware and mindful. For example, if the topic being discussed relates to disability and ableism, then it is the responsibility of the Asian female supervisor to make sure she does not insert her subjugated experiences in the discussion and inadvertently undermine the experiences of the supervisee with the disability. Simultaneously, it would behoove the supervisee to consider the intersecting identities of his female supervisor of color as he shares his experiences as someone with a disability. Then there is the power differential in the supervisor–supervisee relationship regardless of the topic being discussed. This dynamic must also be considered. In general, the person in the position of higher professional rank should take the lead and bear more responsibility to broach difficult dialogues. In the case where the supervisee takes the lead, the supervisor must remain cognizant of and consider the power differential in their response. Ideally, each must meet the other with openness to complexities. This is not the oppression Olympics! It is not productive, helpful, nor healing to try and outdo each other to see who has been oppressed the most. Rather, it is in the spaces of constructive conversations where we can often find common ground.

If you find yourself holding privilege, remember to be patient and humble. Those you are speaking with might be hesitant to open up to you. You may have to earn their trust and show that your intentions are genuine. Privilege can come from a myriad of sources such as the color of your skin, your sex, the language you speak, and the neighborhood you live in. Your privilege can unbeknownst to you, can be in your blind self of the Johari window, and that is the worst place for it. While you can't get rid of your privilege, especially unearned privilege such as race and gender identity, you can move it from the blind window to the known window. By acknowledging your privilege to yourself, you can even own it when embarking on constructive conversations. For example, "Being a man, I don't know what it's like to be a woman in our male-dominated field. But I care sincerely and am committed to doing what I can to advance women's rights in this profession."

Alicia's Turn

One of the family values I was taught again and again as a child was to be polite and respect my elders. My mom constantly reminded me to say my "please" and "thank you." If someone in authority (parent, grandparent, teacher, priest, or police officer) told me something, I was expected to listen respectfully and never talk back!

As you can imagine, one of the barriers I faced as an adult was broaching constructive conversations with someone who was older than me or had authority over me. I found it helpful to acknowledge that doing so was, in many ways, working against the fabric of my childhood.

From there, I have learned to consciously decide when I want to be assertive, reminding myself that dissent is sometimes the right thing to do. As Senator John Lewis wisely advises: in times of injustice, go out and "make good trouble."

Time

Another irrefutable external barrier is the challenge of time. With the hustle and bustle of twenty-first-century living, time for in-depth conversations may feel elusive. Rushing from one agenda item to the next on our calendars can keep us from scheduling constructive conversations at all.

These exchanges can take mental and emotional energy, which also consumes time. Since there are twenty-four hours in a day—no more, no less—no matter what we do, time will always be a constraint, and at best a parameter that influences how and when we take on constructive conversations. Know that with practice, however, engaging in regular constructive conversations can and will become more efficient.

Your Turn

Tick Tock Time Out

You deserve and need to take time out for yourself to work on your constructive conversation skills. Take out your calendar now (whether it's electronic or paper) and find one hour a week to work on practicing, and building up your capacity, for constructive conversations. This can be time on your own or with your accountability buddy—or maybe you can alternate every other week between the two.

You will get more out of this book if you schedule the time to actively engage with the steps. This engagement can involve writing in the journal, practicing our suggested exercises, discussing what you're learning with others, and, as you get further in with the steps, practicing talking and listening to others about your goals.

Turn again to your journal. Now that you are familiar with the common internal and external barriers that can pop up, which resonate most with you? What are your top barriers? List your top five internal barriers on the right side of the page, and you top five external barriers directly next to it on the left. Use this list to both identify your personal barriers and begin to brainstorm what you might be able to do about them.

As you reflect on this list:

- *What can you say to yourself to help challenge or cope with these barriers?*

- *What actions can you take to address them?*

- *What tools from your self-care jar and magic bag can you pull out to help manage these barriers?*

Summary

You've looked in the mirror and examined your blind spots. It's not an easy task, but it's usually an interesting one, to learn more about yourself. Hopefully, you now have a good grasp of what internal and external barriers you may be most commonly up against when pursing constructive conversations.

It can be daunting to see how many obstacles can get in the way but also validating that this is hard work—there are many challenges inherent in working against the paradigm. While identifying barriers is a key step, it's up to you to make sure they don't have the last word.

In the next step, we will discuss the role of values, which we see as the primary antidote to our barriers.

SETTING A VALUE-DRIVEN INTENTION

Values are the heart of the Kim Constructive Conversations Model. Without question, Step 3 is the most important of all the steps and the most critical tool.

In this step, we guide you through the process of setting a value-driven intention. This involves defining the function of values and why we need them, identifying your personal best values, understanding the value of courage, and learning how to practice your values throughout the constructive conversations journey.

At their core, values anchor us when strong emotions, including the fear of uncertain outcomes, threaten to take over. And if you find that you have strayed from your original goals, values will help you find your way back to them.

So get ready. You are about to meet your new best friends. They will serve you well in the most intense and vital parts of this journey.

What Are Values?

By definition, values are those qualities and traits by which we measure our own and others' worth and merit. They are the principles that determine the righteousness of our behaviors and moral standards—our virtues. In his book *Character Matters,* Thomas Lickona defined virtues as "habits of mind, heart, and behavior... [which] develop through deliberate practice." Even if we haven't consciously adopted a particular set of virtues or values, we are constantly in contact with people, systems, and entities that project the importance of one particular value or another. (For the sake of clarity, we will only use the term "values" throughout the remainder of the book to capture the ideas just expressed.)

Over the years, each one of us has likely picked up a collection of values that govern and guide our behaviors, choices, and interactions with others. Even if you are not part of any organized religion and don't adhere to strict cultural practices, the messages of values are inescapable; they are ubiquitous. For example, values can be found in many common cultural proverbs around the globe:

"Laughter is a language everyone understands." (Chad)

"When the sun rises, it rises for everyone." (Cuba)

"Shared joy is double joy; shared sorrow is half a sorrow." (Sweden)

"A beautiful thing is never perfect." (Egypt)

"They tried to bury us. They didn't know we were seeds." (Mexico)

"Fall seven times, stand up eight." (Japan)

These proverbs convey many values, including justice, equity, compassion, and resilience. Similarly, in the United States, there are many proverbs driven by undertones of values, such as "Actions speak louder than words" and "Practice what you preach." And there's "If at first you don't succeed, try, try again," "Practice makes perfect," and "Where there's a will, there's a way." What values do you think these proverbs promote?

Here are a few more for you to think about:

"Every cloud has a silver lining."

"Let bygones be bygones."

"Honesty is the best policy."

"The early bird gets the worm."

"You can't judge a book by its cover."

These common messages that many of us have encountered throughout our lives instruct us on how to behave, and how to understand ourselves and others through their underlying values and assumptions. What values are reflected in the above aphorisms?

Why Do We Need Values?

Values play a critical role not only in guiding our behaviors, but also in directing us to the right decisions at important crossroads in our lives. They challenge us to dig deep and hold on to that which is most aligned with the best versions of ourselves. Values help us to avoid getting hijacked when the ghosts of Pandora's box (the barriers identified earlier) roam wild and threaten to take over. They allow us to take shelter and build strength in the middle of our emotional storms.

This is why we need them. This is why anchoring ourselves in values is so central to having constructive conversations. When the heat becomes too much to bear and our resolve starts to falter, our values remind us to pause, breathe, reconnect with our true intentions, and believe we can and will survive.

Consider the following example: Over a family dinner, you mention that you will be attending an immigrant rights protest and that you hope your family members will join you. Instead of the unanimous agreement you were hoping for, your grandma turns to you and says she believes there should be a ban on all Muslim immigrants because "you never know if one of them could be a terrorist."

Suddenly there is palpable tension around the table, and no one will make eye contact. It's hard to swallow the bite of food in your mouth. You immediately want to shout, "What are you talking about?! We're immigrants too!" But you know better than to raise your voice to elders. Your heart starts pounding and you have lost your appetite. Your emotions of anger and shame are now running amok and you're grappling to regulate. You can't eat or speak and you feel completely derailed. Frantically, you imagine all the ways in which this situation might unfold. You suddenly feel paralyzed by the burden of your impending action and the uncertainty of its outcome.

This is where your values come in. In the midst of this internal emotional storm, you anchor in your personal values. Perhaps those of compassion, forgiveness, faith, and courage. Compassion could help you soften into your anger and shame and connect with the pain that lies beneath. Forgiveness might open, instead of shut down, the now tenuous connection between you and grandma. Faith might assuage your fears of the unknown and uncertain outcomes from this situation. And courage will allow you to be brave enough to do it all.

This may all feel a bit daunting. Not to worry. The task of identifying our values is not a search for existential truth or the ultimate meaning of life. Though should you be open to finding that, by all means please step right in! For the majority of us, the invitation of values into constructive conversations is a means to find important and reliable anchors that can help us weather the inexorable storms and stay connected on the right path for our journey.

Your Turn

In your journal, list some values and/or proverbs that come readily to mind. Think about the kinds of life lessons you were exposed to regularly while growing up. What were some common messages that were communicated to you by your parents, relatives, friends, religious or spiritual community, teachers, or the broader culture? Which of these do you still use when making a decision or facing a problem? Which no longer serve you? (We want to acknowledge that not everyone has the privilege of a safe and loving childhood to refer back to. In this case, we encourage you to consider the family, community, or culture you have chosen or adopted, and from which you received care, support, and acceptance.)

What Are the "Best" Values?

There are many values. None of them are "right" or "wrong." The "best" values are the ones that align with who you are at the core. Since we are all bombarded with so many shoulds and shouldn'ts in our world, finding values that truly align with our true selves can, in and of itself, feel like a daunting task. However, it is not as intimidating as it appears. In fact, if we just stop to consider what is most important in our lives and in our relationships, we can easily identify the values that are most compatible with us.

Here is a list of some common values you can peruse in search of your personal favorites. This is certainly not an exhaustive list, but just some suggestions to get you started.

- Compassion
- Courage
- Dignity
- Empathy
- Faith
- Forgiveness
- Fortitude
- Generosity
- Grace
- Gratitude
- Honesty
- Humility
- Integrity
- Justice
- Love
- Loyalty
- Mercy
- Openness
- Respect
- Self-control
- Trust
- Wisdom

Now, identify at least three values that most resonate with you. This need not be a complete or finite list. You can always add, subtract, change, or even try on another value.

Your Turn

In your journal, you will now build your own tool kit of values to facilitate your navigation and success throughout the constructive conversation venture.

1. What are your personal "best" values? Here are some prompts you might consider in answering this question:

   - *Looking back at the list of proverbs and life lessons you just created, write down what you believe are the underlying values of each proverb or life lesson.*

   - *What qualities do you most admire in a friend or partner?*

   - *What positive traits do others use to describe you?*

   - *Consider one of your most meaningful relationships. What qualities about this relationship do you most value?*

   - *If you are a parent or a caregiver, ask yourself, What are the most important lessons I want my children to learn?*

   - *What traits do you most aspire to or strive for?*

   - *What values guide your life?*

   - *Create your own personal mottos or sayings that you want to guide you in your life.*

2. Now compile a list of your personal "best" values. Keep this list close by as you will be referring to it frequently.

Now you have your own personal tool kit of values—your emergency preparedness kit—which you already know aligns with your true self. You can reach for it when you need it, and trust you have the right tools to help you pull through.

The Importance of Courage

If not already on your personal list of values, please consider adding the value of courage to your list. Maya Angelou writes: "Courage is the most important of all the virtues, because without courage you can't practice any other virtue consistently. You can practice any virtue erratically, but nothing consistently without courage (Graham, 2006)." The value of courage is an indispensable anchor and tool in helping us turn toward and soften into those lurking barriers, as well as into the uncertainties that lie ahead.

What Does It Mean to Be Courageous?

People often make the mistake of believing that those who are courageous must have no fear. Quite the contrary. People who have courage do so in the direct face of fear, anxiety, insecurity, uncertainty, and even calamity. To have constructive conversations on culture and diversity, we have to have courage!

Consider the example of a recently hired employee who identifies as gender queer. This employee notices that there are no all gender or gender-neutral restrooms for them to use at their new place of work. If and when they consider raising this issue with their new employer, it would be an act of courage. Of course, their decision to do so will depend on multiple factors, such as who the employer is, the workplace setting, and the company culture, to name just a few. It would stand to reason that in making the decision to raise this issue, the employee would likely face fear and anxiety about the outcome. Their act of courage would be against the backdrop of possibly being further marginalized, feeling unsafe, or even losing their job. It is their willingness to act despite their fear that makes them courageous.

If you are someone who does not feel like a brave person, you are not alone. When we think of someone who is brave and courageous, we are typically channeling superheroes from the land of Marvel or the exceptional and extraordinary person who makes the five o'clock news because they risked their own life to save the life of a total stranger. No doubt these are acts of bravery, worthy of news and honor. And courage comes in all shapes, sizes, and scales. Most of us are courageous in some way that is significant and meaningful.

Courage for the Average Person

It's much easier to see courage in others than in ourselves. When a teenage nephew tells his adult uncle that he experienced the uncle's comments about cheerleaders during a football game as misogynistic, it is an act of courage. When your Pakistani American friend shares how the travel bans impact his sense of acceptance in his own country of birth, it is an act of courage. When a multiracial son tells his monoracial parents that he does not like being called "mixed," it is an act of courage. When a teacher willingly provides extra accommodations for her student with a disability in spite of inadequate administrative support, it is an act of courage.

Then there is courage within each of us that must be seen, acknowledged, and nurtured. When I trust that my boss will be able to hear my concerns about being penalized for missed work during the observation of my religious holiday, it is an act of courage. When I share that I'm afraid of being perceived as racist, but am willing to engage in difficult racial dialogues, it is an act of courage. When I acknowledge my insecurities about not understanding someone who is culturally different from me, it is an act of courage. When I ask for help, it is an act of courage.

Very simply, courage means the strength to be vulnerable. This definition might sound strange, as we might imagine a courageous person as being fearless and resolute. Rather, courage is a capacity inherent in each of us, superhero or not. Quite simply, it is a mindset, an attitude, and an orientation of the heart that dares to turn toward and soften into our greatest fears, insecurities, and vulnerabilities.

Courage is the chief leader of our troop of values that will allow us to meet our internal and external barriers with compassion, gratitude, wisdom, and grace. This is why we see it as the most central of all values. It allows us to be brave enough to turn inward. In so doing, our capacity to be courageous externally is infinitely magnified.

Your Turn

Refer back to your journal. How are you already brave and courageous?

- *List three things that you did in the last week that you didn't want to do or didn't believe you could do. In each of these events, how were you brave?*

- *List three times you shared something about yourself with another person that was difficult, challenging, or even painful.*

- *Close your eyes and say, "I can be brave. I will be brave. I am brave." How does that feel? Strange? New? Empowering?*

How Do I Practice Values?

Identifying a list of values is one thing, but the "deliberate practice" that Thomas Lickona argues we must develop is an entirely different ball game. There are many avenues to practicing values. Many of us use various methods, most of which are externally generated and motivated (e.g., going to a place of worship or doing something for someone else). However, the most important and difficult approach is the practice of values within ourselves and the mandate to practice them regularly.

Start with Yourself

A famous Spanish proverb offers this: "If you are not good for yourself, how can you be good for others?" This is akin to what we hear routinely whenever we travel by airplane: "Please secure your oxygen mask first before helping those around you."

Think about these messages literally and figuratively. No matter how noble your intention in helping someone sitting next to you, you cannot be effective if you yourself have not first secured your own mask. In your oxygen-deprived state, your ability to help your co-passenger is invariably compromised, no matter how honorable your intentions. Similarly, if we have not faced our own fears and insecurities about topics like classism and transphobia, how are we supposed to hold space when the fears and insecurities of someone else come hurtling at us? We start by securing our own oxygen masks.

CASE STUDY

In the context of having constructive conversations and practicing values, this means applying those values to ourselves first and foremost. Consider the example of Marisol, an American-born working mother of Mexican ancestry, who recently added compassion to her tool kit of values. Even though her reconnection to this value has been relatively recent, she also realized that it actually has been with her throughout her life.

As far back as she can remember, she was inundated with messages to be compassionate to others. Everywhere she turned, there were irrefutable messages about how "good" girls are "nice" girls who always help and take care of others first. She also grew up in a collectivistic family culture, where the needs of others and the greater whole always prevailed. Thus, it was very easy to develop compassion for others. But against this backdrop, the idea of having compassion for herself was always effortful for Marisol.

She still struggles with meeting everyone else's needs first. However, she is beginning to understand more and more the need to practice and grow her value of self-compassion. Having self-compassion is not only caring for herself, it is also caring for others with whom she comes into contact: her partner, children, coworkers, friends, and even strangers. If she is able to secure her self-compassion mask, when she finds herself in situations that warrant constructive conversations—e.g., when her coworker makes a sexist comment about her wardrobe; when her child is automatically placed in an English as a Second Language class; when a new acquaintance asks where she's from—she is better able to meet whatever challenges arise and remain aligned with her value-driven intentions.

Do It Daily

Building and strengthening any value means practicing it daily. Learning any new skill requires patience and practice. Incorporating values into our lives is no exception. As such, we encourage you to start practicing right away. Do it daily. You don't need to wait for a crisis. In fact, developing good habits now will help you when you need them most.

For Marisol, practicing self-compassion involves going for a bike ride, getting her kids out the door with minimal nagging (sometimes), asking for help when she's feeling overwhelmed, speaking up when someone commits a microaggression, and even receiving, with appreciation, feedback when she herself commits a microaggression. When she practices the value of self-compassion, she can comfort herself when she is hijacked by feelings of anger, frustration, resentment, or other barriers that could impede her goals. She can also stand firmly as someone else's Pandora's box opens, as their feelings of inadequacy, anxiety, anger, fear, and pain erupt. Anchored in the values of self-compassion and courage, she doesn't have to abort mission or unleash her emotional defenses. She can simply turn toward and soften into that powerful space between herself and the other person.

Here are three ways that can help you integrate and practice living your values in your daily life.

1. Practice deep-breathing exercises to help ground you into a given value.

    Instructions: Come up with a plan to do this exercise daily. Pick a specific time of the day—maybe as soon as you wake up and before getting out of bed, or just before you go to sleep in the evening. Any block of five minutes or so will do. If you think it will help remind you and keep you accountable, enter it into your calendar or set an alarm. Start with a commitment to do it every day for one week; after that time, evaluate the effectiveness of your plan. Maybe you need to pick a different time of day or adjust the duration to make it sustainable.

Find a quiet space. Get comfortable. Relax your body. Start at the top of your head and gradually move down to the tip of your toes. As you scan your body, imagine the different parts sinking effortlessly and deeply into the chair you are sitting on or the floor you are lying on. If you are standing, one at a time, tighten and then fully relax each muscle group, from your head to your toes.

Now, take a deep diaphragmatic (belly) breath in, full of your chosen value (maybe courage, trust, love). Hold for a count of three. Drink in that value. Then slowly breathe out any barriers (maybe fear, anger). Breathe in value, breathe out barrier. Do this for ten rounds of inhalation and exhalation.

As this exercise becomes more familiar and you begin to notice the benefits, do it more often. You don't need to limit yourself to once a day—practice as often and for as long as you like. Since your breath is always with you, there's no need to worry about packing it and taking it with you. Do it at work, while waiting in line or washing dishes, just before a presentation, during a disagreement, and so forth. Venture out and experience the many ways this exercise can work in your favor.

As you develop a regular practice, you will begin to notice positive changes in your general mood—most likely an overall sense of calm and grounding.

2. Use guided imagery exercises that invite you to visualize your values.

Instructions: Using your own imagination or a prerecorded tape, generate an image or listen to a guided visualization. You should reserve at least five to ten minutes for this exercise. As before, find a regular time and place to practice. A time that works well for most people is first thing in the morning or just before bedtime. This is often when the house is quiet and surrounding activity level is at a minimum. When you have secured a regular time and space, find a posture that will work best for you (sitting on a chair, lying down on your bed or the floor). Before starting the guided visualization, spend two to three minutes getting into a comfortable position and systematically relaxing your body. You might use the body scan described above to reach this state of relaxation.

You are now ready to begin. Below is an example of a guided visualization. Feel free to use this one, modify it, or create your own. Remember to commit to doing this exercise daily. If you'd like, and time permitting, we encourage you to do this and the previous breathing exercise together, one following the other.

Imagine you are on a beach. As you walk along the soft sand, you come to a gift-wrapped box. It has your name on it. You instantly feel excited to open it. At first the box seems empty, but as you look closer, you see your value of [insert your value here]. What does it look like? Perhaps you decide to pick it up. What does it feel like? Notice the color, the size, and the texture. How heavy is it? What sounds does it make?

Now imagine that you want this value to join you on your walk. For some reason, you know it would be a trusted and valuable companion. You begin to walk with [insert your value here] by your side. You already feel different—more grounded and relaxed. As it turns out, [insert your value here] has nowhere else to go and is able to stay by your side as long as you need. Knowing this, you feel even more grounded, reassured, and hopeful.

As you build your guided imagery skills, we encourage you to incorporate it beyond your usual practice time and place. This might include during times of stress or difficulty. Maybe during rush-hour traffic, when you start noticing your agitation rising. (Of course, if you are driving keep your eyes open!) If you don't have a prerecorded tape of your guided visualization, you can simply conjure up a still image of it.

If you have practiced this skill enough, you will have developed a familiar mental image: the beach with its clear blue skies, warm soft sand between your toes, and your box of values tucked under your arm. Go to that image. Allow yourself to bathe in what the image represents.

Now come back to your present moment, in the middle of rush hour. How does your guided imagery influence your agitation? Can you feel it melting away? You can even enhance this by practicing your diaphragmatic breathing. Breathe in value, breathe out agitation. You are still sitting in traffic, nothing has changed. But notice how the simple practice of imagery and breathing helps you experience this stressful event in an entirely different way.

Do this for any other events or situations that cause discomfort or distress. Practice it as often as you can and want. The more you do, the better you will get, and the greater the benefits.

3. Practice positive affirmations or self-statements that help you embrace your value.

Instructions: Like the previous two exercises, this one will not take too much of your time. A few minutes, at most, is all you need. If done regularly, it can reap many benefits. So commit to practicing these affirmations daily. It might feel silly in the beginning, but stick with it. With repetition, it will feel more natural and comfortable.

Again, schedule a time to practice. Maybe as you get ready in the morning. Or during an afternoon break at work. Or as you prepare to settle in for the night with a cup of tea.

There are also numerous methods for doing this. For example, you might pick one affirmation every day from a list, such as the one below. Or you might pick one and practice the same one every day for a week. Or you might even pick multiple affirmations to practice daily.

Whatever you decide, we recommend that you first come up with a list of affirmations that resonate with you. The list need not be long. If you're having a hard time getting started, feel free to search for other ideas on the Internet.

Finally, decide how you will practice. Maybe you will recite the affirmation slowly and deliberately as you stand in front of a mirror. Or maybe you will write it down in your schedule book or as a reminder in your phone and read it quietly to yourself throughout the day. Be creative. There is no "right" or "wrong" way to do this. Make it your own.

To help you get started, here are some examples you might consider:

> *It's okay to make mistakes.*
>
> *It's okay to be scared.*
>
> *I am brave enough to speak my truth.*
>
> *I trust that my pain will be heard.*
>
> *I have hope that my missteps will be forgiven.*
>
> *I can be honest.*
>
> *I will be brave.*
>
> *I have faith.*

As you grow your familiarity and strength with this exercise, expand its use to other settings and situations. This might include challenging exchanges with others. Maybe as you share difficult news with a friend. Or as you prepare to apologize for a mistake you made (e.g., assuming someone's sexual orientation, gender, or race). You might tell yourself, *It's okay to be nervous. I can be honest. Owning my mistakes is important.* As before, you can additionally incorporate diaphragmatic breathing, as well as guided imagery. Breathe in value, breathe out anxiety.

Learning to have constructive conversations is a process. Taking this small but important step will prepare you well for when you plan to have the full constructive conversation experience.

Your Turn

Refer again to your journal. Take out your list of personal "best" values. Reread it. Now ask yourself:

- *In what ways have I practiced each of these values for myself?*

- *How often do I practice these values for myself?*

- *What makes it easier or harder to do this?*

- *How can I do it more often?*

- *When I am able to practice these values for myself, what is the impact?*

Seeing Clear to Our Values

As mentioned in Step 2, barriers can abound when having constructive conversations. Among others, these include difficult emotions such as anger, outrage, and fear.

The goal in setting a value-driven intention is not to eliminate these barriers. In reality, so much of our suffering comes from the stories we tell ourselves. And our stories about our vulnerabilities can bring us tremendous pain. As we try to avoid the pain and grasp for something different, we can find ourselves in an endless tailspin. This does not feel good and it serves no one, least of all ourselves.

The goal, then, is to allow our values to help us orient toward and soften into these barriers. In turn, they will bring greater insight into our internal experiences and enhance our ability to have constructive conversations.

Meet Elizabeth and Manuel: Constructive Conversations with Strangers

Let's consider the case of Elizabeth. Elizabeth was enjoying the afternoon with her five-year-old son Jason at their local shopping mall. Elizabeth's wife, Mónica, was at work and unable to join them for the family outing.

A store clerk, Manuel, smiled at the mother-son duo, and engaged Jason in conversation. Manuel complimented Jason's good behavior, and commented, "I bet your dad is very proud of you, little man." Elizabeth was flustered and angry by the store clerk's assumption about their family.

Activated but not surprised, she looked down protectively at her son to see his reaction. She struggled about whether or not to respond to Manuel. She was unsure how much attention she wanted to bring to this interaction with her son watching. Her initial impulse was to yell at or disparage Manuel for his heterosexist and sexist assumptions. But then what? She knew she would not feel any less angry or disappointed.

Elizabeth was also aware that she did not want to disrespect Manuel as a man of color, and so was cautious about how to proceed. Ultimately, Elizabeth opted to engage with this stranger, because she felt that keeping quiet would invalidate her identity, dishonor her wife, and potentially communicate to Jason that having two moms is something to hide—or that for little boys, affirmation from fathers is somehow more valuable than that from mothers.

Given Elizabeth's goal to speak up and address Manuel's assumptions, if she identified and integrated her values of strength, hope, and perseverance in this process, she would exponentially enhance the possibility of having a successful constructive conversation. These values could accompany her initial frustration, disappointment, and anger—allaying their intensity without compromising their validity. These barriers could thus be less likely to deter Elizabeth's efforts to speak the truth of her family. As she anchors herself in her values, maybe through a breathing exercise and imagery visualization, she reconnects to the pain of how often she has encountered, and will continue to encounter, prejudice. She is able to tap into strength and perseverance to dig deep, because she knows her truth deserves to be spoken. In channeling the value of hope, she can realize the wish to be heard for herself, her wife, and their son.

Guided by these values, Elizabeth is able to turn to Manuel—not with an untempered reaction to his microaggression but rather with an opportunity to heal herself and deepen her understanding with others.

Try retelling the story about your barriers through the lens of your values. Maybe your barrier of anger, viewed through values such as love and mercy, might bring a deeper sense of understanding and softness into your pain, as someone targeted by bigotry and oppression. Maybe your value of compassion can cradle the shame you might feel about your privilege. Or maybe the value of courage can both embrace and disarm your fear of being rejected and alienated if you disclose your true identity and experience.

What is *your* value-driven story? How does it feel? Does it allow you to better travel the journey toward constructive conversations?

Your Turn

You too can do what Elizabeth did. Frustration, disappointment, anger, and pain, though absolutely real and legitimate, do not have to run the show—because in the end, they will not help you move successfully toward your goals. Value-driven intentions, on the other hand, will.

So how can you use values to guide your experience through situations like the one Elizabeth encountered? Start living your life according to your personal values. Fundamental to many cultural traditions is the understanding and practice of value-driven living.

For the purposes of having constructive conversations, here are some suggestions to help you incorporate values into your daily life.

1. To start, create a personal mission statement for yourself. What or who is most important to you? How do you want to travel and navigate your life's journey? What legacy do you want to leave behind? These are not simple questions. They will require some time and thought to answer. Be patient and give yourself the space you need. Remember, you can always

change your statement as you move through this process. A working statement is just as good as any other. In fact, a draft will allow you to think it through more deeply, without pressure to get it "right" or make it perfect. Your statement can be short or long, general or detailed, and original or borrowed. Come up with whatever works for you, whatever rings true, and whatever speaks most clearly from the heart.

If you are new to personal mission statements, here are a few examples to help you get started: "To love and be loved"; "To not be afraid of mistakes or failures"; "It is my mission to live my life with integrity, honesty, and compassion. To follow my dreams relentlessly. And to love fiercely." One of the most well-known mission statements is the Serenity Prayer, offered to those struggling to fight addiction: "God, grant me the serenity to accept the things I cannot change, the courage to change the things I can, and the wisdom to know the difference."

What do you notice in all these examples? What values are included or assumed in your personal mission statement?

2. Now that you have a living version of your personal mission statement, get ready to implement it into your daily life. How? Given the goal of having constructive conversations, let's start with your relationships. Identify one or two relationships that are important to you. Maybe your marriage or partnership, or a child, family member, friend, or work colleague. What about your connection with this person is important to you? How do you ideally want to engage with this person? What do you ultimately want to foster with them? How does your personal mission statement relate to this relationship?

For the next week, commit to interacting with your important person through the lens of your personal mission statement. Bring the values of that mission to the foreground. Doing so will allow you to connect more meaningfully, no matter what the topic or situation. Why? Because it will be your heart responding and receiving, not your intellectual interpretations or defenses. Values are the matters of our tender hearts.

So, try it. Have your personal mission statement close by—or better yet, memorize it. Repeat your mission and keep it actively in mind as you interact with your important person—as you share a meal together, talk about work projects, inquire about their day at school, or even during a disagreement or conflict.

What happens when you do this? Evaluate the overall impact at the end of the week and decide what to do next. Maybe continue for another week with the same person? Maybe expand to include another important person in your life? Harmonious relationships are not magical. They require hard work. They also require that you ground in what is most important: your values.

3. Bring values into everyday interactions. Don't reserve values only for those situations that are uncomfortable, stressful, or downright difficult. Instead, use them in daily interactions, to experience and harness their power. This includes seemingly mundane exchanges, such as when we say "good morning" or "thank you" to whomever. If filtered through the lens of love, and gratitude, a simple gesture of greeting can have deeper meaning and influence on all involved. Think about it. An out-of-habit "good morning" is generally received and reciprocated without much plan or thought. Depending on which side of the bed you woke up on, you might not even mean it! But you say it nevertheless, out of habit or sense of obligation. At most it's good manners and common courtesy. But what if, instead, you wish someone a good morning because you remember you love them and are grateful for them? Even though it's the same two words that are spoken, because they are delivered from a place of active love and gratitude, they are going to be experienced differently for both the speaker and the receiver. It's more than

being sincere with our words. It's about understanding why we are speaking those words and how they are aligned with what is most important to us.

Try it for yourself. Start slow. Identify a habit-driven interaction you regularly engage in. Maybe it's a simple greeting such as "good morning," "good night," "hi," "bye," or "how are you?" Or a common expression such as "thank you" or "please." The next time you find yourself in any of these common interactions, speak from and through your values (e.g., kindness, respect, curiosity, love, or gratitude). For example, you say "thank you" to the driver as you step off the bus because you are grateful for his service; you are grateful he drove you and the others safely to your destination. You say "good night" to a coworker as you leave work because you really hope she has a restful and enjoyable evening; she worked diligently all day and you wish her well. Since opportunities to engage in these greetings and gestures are plentiful, you can practice every day! Notice how your mood and the quality of your day shift. You might even notice the impact your value-driven behaviors have on those around you.

Your Turn

Turn once more to your journal.

1. Take out the list of barriers from Step 2 and the list of your personal "best" values. For each of the barriers, identify a value on your list that might be used to help mitigate the specific barrier.

2. Now imagine the constructive conversation you'd like to have one day soon. Write down as much detail as possible about this future scenario, including your goals. What is the link between your values and goals? What is the role your values might play in you actualizing your goals?

Summary

Identifying values or using them to address our barriers might not be easy. But we are all capable of it.

Please take your time in setting your values. Be patient. You don't want a quick solution—that usually only leads to bigger problems later. Remember, your barriers, including strong emotions and fear of uncertain outcomes, require your time, patience, and care to work through them.

Now that you have set a goal, identified your barriers, and set a value-driven intention, you are ready to move onward. In the steps ahead, emotional storms might await you. Remember to keep coming back, again and again, to your values. They will be your most faithful, reliable, and effective guides and companions.

SET THE STAGE

Up until now you have learned that constructive communication begins internally, with yourself. Only when you have your goals established (Step 1), barriers identified (Step 2), and best values called into practice (Step 3), can you approach the other person.

In this step, you will learn how to set an effective stage (Step 4) for your conversation. Setting the stage is crucial. In the following pages we share suggestions on how to open up the conversation with effective wording and delivery that is grounded in the core values you have already identified. We will give you examples and scripts of what you can say when starting a constructive conversation.

We'll also help guide you through making important decisions about *how* and *when* to deliver your message. Delivery matters, so the style and timing of your message can be just as important as what you say. By building self-awareness regarding your natural communication style—What is the natural pace, volume, and style of your voice? What nonverbal communication do you use? How do your family and cultural background influence your communication style?—you can make conscious choices about how you want to broach a given topic.

Anchored with your identified values, you are now ready to set the stage for the conversation to come. Let's get started!

Open Wide!

To successfully set the stage is to introduce what you are about to say in a way that maximizes how it will be received. Simple, introductory sentences are openers for what's to come. How you frame these openers, including when and where, are other ingredients for setting a successful stage. While the opener does not take long to articulate, it is powerful. Setting the stage with a successful opener dramatically shifts and shapes the way the constructive conversation transpires.

If a constructive conversation is a delicious dinner, setting the stage is the tableware. Imagine serving dinner without a plate, utensils, or a napkin. The guest may eat the food, but they will probably dislike the dining experience. Don't count on that person coming back either. Similarly, initiating a constructive conversation without setting the stage (without setting the table) will likely leave a bad taste in the person's mouth, take them off guard, and get everything off to a poor start.

Setting the stage helps prepare your family member, friend, or whoever it is you are about to speak with, and gives them an opportunity to get ready. You have already spent time preparing yourself: setting your personalized goals, anticipating barriers, and identifying your values. However, the person you are speaking to might not know this is coming. Setting the stage gives the person a heads-up. Up until this point, you have focused on introspection and looking inward. You now focus outward; you verbalize and make explicit what has, up until this point, been internal.

Your Turn

Turn to your journal. Reflect on the ways you may have consciously or unconsciously set the stage for previous high-stakes conversations with various people in your life. You may already have experienced delivering big, new, or difficult news. Perhaps you've had to fire somebody? Told a partner about an unexpected pregnancy? Or initiated a breakup? For such situations:

- *How did you set the stage for these conversations?*
- *How did you begin?*
- *What did you say?*
- *How did you say it?*
- *When and where did you say it?*

Let Your Values Set the Stage

Effective and persuasive openers are anchored in your chosen values. When starting a constructive conversation with someone, we recommend choosing opening words that show you are coming from a genuine place. This approach allows you to be transparent and vulnerable about your intentions. After all, isn't that why you are doing this in the first place? To be real! To talk to someone heart to heart. Let's get started by going back to your values and anchoring your openers there.

If your top values are hope and honesty, you may start with "I feel hopeful that we can talk openly about what just happened." If you are anchoring yourself in faith, you may choose to say, "I am going to dig deep here and go out on a limb." In both of these examples, the phrasing reflects the core values. Setting the stage gives you, the initiator of the conversation, an opportunity to slow down and verbalize the conscious intention you are about to set. Choosing openers that share your values in this way signals to the listener that you are coming from a sincere place. Your thoughtfully selected opening words, in turn, invite the listener to experience your message in that light. When done correctly, setting the stage increases the chances that true connection will occur between you and the person you are talking to, because it increases the chances that your message will be received with openness.

Setting the stage must be done in a way that is genuine to the speaker. The listener will be able to sniff out inauthenticity. If they perceive the opener is forced or not sincere, then instead of their guard going down, their defenses will come up. This is the opposite of the purpose of the opener. That does not mean that you can't try a new way of saying something. Instead, it means you need to choose openers that reflect your true thoughts and feelings.

Here are some suggestions for developing an effective opener.

1. Use "I" statements that are brief and concise.

2. Use your core values to guide your word choice. For example, "I have faith that together we can talk through this" or "I trust in the strength of our relationship and know we can handle talking about this." Choose words that reflect your openness and show that what you are about to do is personal. Examples include: "I hope," "I wish," "I want," and "I would like."

3. Invite the listener to join you in a mutual engagement or exchange, such as "I would like to try something new here and hope you'll join me."

4. Don't verbalize an opener that signals bad news is to come. Opening in this way (e.g., the classic "I think you better sit down") typically alarms the listener, keys them up, and increases tension before they even hear the core of the message.

Your Turn

In your journal, using the format described above, write a few of your own individualized openers. Choose people in your life that you want to broach issues with. These do not have to be about culture or diversity per se, but they should be topics that you anticipate may get some pushback or defensiveness from the other person. For example, in situations like the following:

1. Your friend invites you to hang out, but you're not feeling up to it.

2. Your boss asks you do to do something you disagree with.

3. Someone illegally pulls their car into a parking space for people with disabilities and you want to confront them about it.

4. Your family member forgets to do something you asked them to do (for the tenth time!).

These can be touchy situations, and effective openers will help to facilitate more constructive dialogue.

All-Purpose Openers

In addition to showing you how to personalize your opener to each situation at hand, we also want to give you some strong, concise examples of setting the stage. We believe that these openers introduce the content of the constructive conversation in a way that shows your intentions are to engage with sincerity.

- "I'm not exactly sure how to say this…" (core values: courage, humility)

- "I hope you will consider taking a risk with me…" (core values: hope, courage, bravery)

- "I'd like to explore doing something different here and would love for you to join me…" (core value: curiosity)

- "I'd like to offer my personal perspective here, and I hope you will hear me out…" (core values: curiosity, creativity, hope)

As you read, keep the following questions in mind: *Can I see myself saying this? Which openers feel most like me? How would I change this opener to better reflect my voice?*

Now that you've seen some examples, we'll examine the nuances and unique qualities of each of these starters.

"I'm not exactly sure how to say this..."

Recall Elizabeth, who was shopping with her young son, Jason. Elizabeth was flustered, disappointed, and angered by the store clerk's assumption about their family. Initially, she struggled about whether or not to speak up to Manuel, the store clerk. Ultimately, Elizabeth opted to engage with this stranger because she felt that keeping quiet would invalidate her identity, dishonor her wife, and potentially communicate to Jason that having two moms is something to hide.

Elizabeth set the stage by saying, "I'm not exactly sure how to say this, and in fact it's hard for me to say. But I think it's important that I do, and so I hope you'll hear me out." Elizabeth's opener suggests values of strength, hope, and perseverance. Through the word choice in her opener, Elizabeth acknowledges that this is a challenging interaction for her, and she doesn't have it all figured out. Yet she is also communicating that she values what she is doing, is not taking it lightly, and is hopeful that she will be listened to. By setting the stage, Elizabeth gives Manuel some insight about her state of mind and intentions. Elizabeth's approach reflects how persuasive openers can have a direct link to our identified values.

"I hope you will consider taking a risk with me..."

By beginning with "I *hope* you will *consider* taking a risk *with me*," you are acknowledging that you do not exactly know how this interaction is going to work out but you are going to try it anyway. This opening statement means you are knowingly and willingly trying out something that is uncertain. You are signaling to the listener that you are about to articulate something that requires you to be brave or courageous.

Underneath that bravery may be fear, worry, or even dread. While the recipient doesn't know exactly, they do get a heads-up that whatever you are saying might be hard for you to say. In essence, this opener highlights your humanness. It signals to the listener that you are not a preacher about to deliver a sermon. You are not an arrogant know-it-all who is going to shame them. You are not a professor giving a lecture. Instead, you are one human being trying to reach out to another.

Introducing the word "hope" shows that you value what you are about to say. We hope for things we care about. We hope for outcomes that we believe will be positive. Therefore, adding the word "hope" communicates your optimism for a successful outcome. Hope also shows your humanity and vulnerability. We rarely share our true hopes with people we don't trust. When we do, we can feel vulnerable. While you don't exactly know what will transpire next, you are hopeful for what will happen.

The opener "I hope you will consider taking a risk with me" also invites the listener to join in on the conversation. This delivery gives some agency to the recipient, allowing them to decide to accept the risk or decline it. Using this approach decreases the chances that the listener will feel threatened by a conversation they did not initiate. The invitation is to join a collaborative connection and a mutual exploration that can lead to healing.

When broaching a constructive conversation with a family member, the risk element might feel especially threatening. Our family members are typically the people we have known the longest, and so we tend to be especially invested in keeping these relationships as harmonious as possible. This new style can take some time to adjust to, and it may take some practice to feel natural and be received that way.

"I'd like to explore doing something different and would love for you to join me..."

This opener communicates to the listener that this is new territory for both of you. By expressing you'd like to do something, you are starting with a preference rather than a demand. The exploration you are proposing is a collaborative one, which suggests it is not already predefined. Letting the person you are talking to know that you are in the moment with what you are saying and that things are not completely predetermined can really help them hear your message as well.

By definition, exploring is not stagnant or set in stone. This statement acknowledges that this is a different way of talking, while continuing to integrate a desire for mutuality.

"I'd like to offer my personal perspective here, and I hope you will hear me out..."

Another way to offer an exploratory approach is to situate yourself in your experience and your opinion. You can acknowledge your own subjectivity in a way that upholds its own innate value, while also underscoring it as just that: *your* view. This opener addresses that this statement is not fact per se, but a personal take on something.

The opener also introduces the idea that disagreement may occur; the communicator's vocal qualities and delivery of this statement can also show that disagreement alone does not have to be an explosive thing. Openers tend to have the quality of "metatalking"—that is, talking about what and how you will be communicating.

Your Turn

Now that you've learned about some common openers that work effectively, go to your journal to take note of the openers that resonate with you the most.

In addition to the openers described above, here are a dozen more to choose from:

1. "I've been thinking about something for a while, and I'd like to take a chance and open up about it."

2. "I'm not sure I have the right words for what I'm feeling, but I'm going to try. So here it goes. Thanks for bearing with me."

3. "This is hard for me to say, but I'm hopeful that we can talk through this together."

4. "This is really painful for me to talk about, because I've experienced some trauma around it. That said, I feel it's important for me to talk with you about it."

5. "There's something really important to me that I'd like to share with you."

6. "I am going to dig deep here and share with you what's coming up."

7. "I feel confident that we can talk openly about what just happened."

8. "I have faith that together we can talk through this."

9. "I'm nervous to bring this up, and I hope you'll hear me out."

10. "I would like to address something that's a bit sensitive, but I know we can handle talking about this."

11. "I've been hearing some rumors that I'm not sure are true, so I wanted to come to you directly."

12. "While we might not be on the same page about what I'm about to say, I hope you can find it in your heart to hear me out."

Now that you've identified your favorite openers and written your own, it's time for more practice. All of this practicing is to get these openers to feel more like a part of your natural way of talking.

Think about situations in your life where you'd like to express something new or hard. Maybe you want to communicate that you want change? Or perhaps you want to express your feelings to a person? Try using your openers to initiate conversations like these:

1. You really like the person you are dating and want to move the relationship to the next level.

2. Your partner has been traveling for work more and more frequently, and it's taking a toll on you and your relationship.

3. Your coworker hasn't been doing their share on the project you are working on.

4. Your friend disclosed to other people something you shared with them in confidence.

Setting the Stage: Beyond Content

Delivery of a message matters. Along with choosing the words, how you say them counts just as much. Consider a message delivered in a monotone. It leaves the recipient confused as to what the person is actually trying to say. Think about text messaging: frequently, it leads to miscommunication. A text is misinterpreted because the emotion in a voice can't be deciphered. You read a text from someone you are newly dating and you are left wondering, *Was that meant to be funny?* You text someone, "How are you doing?" When they respond "Fine," you're not sure what conclusions to draw, with no emotional cues. It could be "Fine, thank you so much for asking, you're so kind" or "Fine, I'm not going to say any more because I don't want to encourage this conversation."

There are many other examples. You get the point. The feelings in one's voice strongly impact the person being spoken to. The listener will interpret and react to your vocal qualities. A kind, gentle voice can turn a neutral comment into a loving one and a critical comment into a palatable one.

By paying attention to your natural style of speaking, you can make deliberate decisions about how you say something that will in turn directly impact how the message will be received. In other words, you can significantly increase the chances of setting the stage successfully by having good self-awareness and being open to modifying your style if needed.

We want to be crystal clear on this point. We are not asking you to be fake or disingenuous. We are not asking you to change who you are. And especially for those of you initiating conversations with people who have current, or even historical power over you, we are definitely not encouraging "tone policing." We understand firsthand the pain marginalized communities have undergone, including demands to mute and alter our true selves again and again to be heard, accepted, and respected in this world. Above all, do not compromise yourself or your integrity when setting the stage.

What we do want to do is give you tools that you can use or not use, based on your needs and judgment. These tools are designed to help embolden and empower your true voices to be heard.

Now, let's consider delivery variables that may help you set the stage effectively. These variables include the quality, volume, and pacing of your voice; nonverbal communication; and timing.

Voice

Consider the following tips for setting the stage:

1. Use a calm, kind, and steady quality in your voice.

2. Keep your volume within a medium zone.

3. Set a deliberate, measured, and even slow pace of words.

We are not asking you to be a robot, or to be someone you are not. However, think about someone who is delivering a speech, asking for a favor, or even proposing marriage. It typically takes some forethought, preparation, and intentionality as to how they want the words to come out. A constructive conversation is no different. Apply these three tips while also adapting them to the person with whom you are speaking. If you are talking to someone with a hearing difficulty, for example, you may need to raise your volume further. Use these tips with flexibility for the situation at hand.

The way we each express ourselves is a very personal matter. In fact, we debated whether to include this section, because we do not want you to feel invalidated in any way. Women, people of color, LGBTQ folks, immigrants, and many more marginalized communities have been given many negative messages about their genuine self-expression. "You're too loud." "You're too soft-spoken." "Stop being so dramatic!" "I can't understand your accent." "You're too aggressive." "You're too flamboyant." "Can you tone it down a bit?" Micro- and macroaggressions such as these definitely sting and wound.

Systems and people in positions of power and privilege continue to play critical roles in constructing, denigrating, invalidating, and silencing marginalized voices. No doubt, different voices are judged and treated differently, with dominant voices—those with economic, social, and cultural status and capital—being privileged over others.

Consider the stereotype of the loud, angry Black woman. We can agree that "soft" and "loud," as well as the ways emotions are verbalized, are strongly influenced by cultural norms and the way our families raise us. Yet we see throughout history that disparaging stereotypes have been used to silence the oppressed, so that if and when a Black woman does speak, we are conditioned to invalidate her—expecting her to be loud and angry, whether or not she is indeed loud or angry. This is most certainly the definition of privilege—to not question what feels natural and automatic for the person holding privilege. So we encourage you to remind yourself that we all exist against the backdrop of context, both present and historical.

We want to be very clear that in order for constructive conversations to be legitimate, honest, and effective, we must be brave enough to be ourselves and brave enough to not judge others through our subjective lens.

Alicia's Turn

My voice is naturally high-pitched. When speaking on the phone with someone for the first time, I am often mistaken for being much, much younger then I am. I've been advised to deepen my voice before interviews and other important work calls.

Initially, this feedback stung! I was told that while I was very qualified and competent, if someone didn't know me yet the sound of my voice might suggest inexperience and immaturity. This advice came from people who genuinely cared about me and my future. Yet it led to me feeling increasingly self-conscious about my voice, which I already had some insecurity about.

Ultimately, I decided to apply the advice when I agree it will be helpful for my goals in a first impression, and to not worry about it when I want to just talk without self-monitoring in this way.

When Voice Can't Be Heard

When done without care, communication such as texting (or emailing) can lead to much confusion and even unintended relationship disconnections. As mentioned above, it is very hard to decipher feelings, nuance, and intention with this way of communicating. Therefore, we don't encourage you to have constructive conversations over instant messaging.

However, if you are trying to set an effective stage via text, email, or IM, here are some do's and don'ts.

Do:

- Ask if the person is free and has some time to chat.

- Use emoticons to show the feeling involved, especially if you think the recipient might not be sure about the intention of your message.

- Use words to explain things like pauses, in the midst of a conversation. For example, "I'm not going to text for a bit, because I need time to think."

- Slow down. The beauty of text messages is that you do usually have time to collect your thoughts and respond thoughtfully. Take advantage of this and slow down to really think about your response. Perhaps even let someone you trust read your message before sending. If what you've written does include an unintended vibe, your proofreader can help point that out.

- Check in and clarify the meaning of someone's text if it rubs you the wrong way.

Don't:

- Assume the worst when reading someone's ambiguous text messaging.

- Read into it if you don't get a reply. Technology can fail us, texts can go missing or be sent to the wrong person, and people get busy.

Nonverbal Communication

Nonverbal communication is equally vital to effectively setting the stage. This includes facial expressions, eye contact, and posture. An exasperated sigh, rolling one's eyes, crossing one's arms, and tapping one's foot can all signal loud messages of annoyance, frustration, and agitation, without any words being spoken. On the other hand, appropriate eye contact and an open body posture indicate that someone is present and cares about the conversation they are trying to have.

Therapists in training are often asked to record their sessions with consenting clients. This method of training is an invaluable tool. Once they get over the initial discomfort of viewing themselves, student clinicians soon realize the critical role their nonverbal language plays in working with clients, including establishing a strong rapport. The trick is remembering that just as we as therapists rely on reading others' nonverbal language to understand where they are coming from, our clients are also reading our nonverbal language when communicating with us. The latter is harder to monitor since we usually can't see our own nonverbal communication.

Recall Elizabeth's words to the store clerk Manuel as an example of how nonverbal communication matters. She told Manuel, "I'm not exactly sure how to say this, and in fact it's hard for me to say. But I think it's important that I do, and so I hope you'll hear me out." Envision Elizabeth saying this to Manuel in a couple of different scenarios. In the first, she leans in, with her shoulders less than a foot away from Manuel's body, glares with her eyebrows furrowed, and uses her pointer finger to single out Manuel. In the second scenario, Elizabeth is holding her son's hand with her left hand, while her right hand remains at her side, except when her palm naturally comes to her heart when she says the phrase "hard for me." Her body stance remains open and she faces Manuel the entire time she sets the stage with her opening statements. Even if these two scenarios were on mute, and you could not hear Elizabeth's words, you could still perceive how Elizabeth is feeling and detect the energy she is directing toward Manuel. That is how loudly our nonverbal communication comes across.

It is also paramount to keep in mind that what feels appropriate and comfortable can vary greatly across cultures. For example, some cultures perceive direct eye contact as essential for respect, while other see it as a sign of disrespect, especially when addressing elders. Some cultural norms support the importance of personal space when speaking with another person, while other cultures encourage close physical proximity. Therefore, acknowledge and anticipate how your style for nonverbal communication aligns and diverges with the person you are speaking to.

How do your family and culture influence your verbal and nonverbal communication style? The next time you have dinner with your family, put on your detective hat, and pay attention. What are the go-to mannerisms of each person at the table? How do their nonverbals influence how you receive whatever it is they are telling you? Do you share any of these family traits?

To communicate that you are open and inviting engagement when setting the stage, consider the following do's and don'ts:

Do:

- Face the person.

- Make good, appropriate eye contact.

- Keep your body stance open and facing the person you are talking to.

- Mirror the other person's body language to communicate that you are connected to them. For example, if they are leaning in, and you also lean in, this can bring balance and intimacy to the conversation.

Don't:

- Cross your arms, which suggests you are defensive or closed off to what the other person is saying.

- Frown.

- Furrow your brow.

- Look down at your nails, play with your hair, fidget.

Some of these suggestions may not be practical for you. Certain disabilities and conditions, such as Tourette syndrome or other tic disorders, cerebral palsy, and social anxiety, to name a few, make some of these suggestions null and void. If you find yourself in this position, please try considering the larger essence of this section, rather than the specific tips. If you do have control over your nonverbal cues, use them to let the person you are approaching know that you are coming with good intentions.

Your Turn

Now let's put some of what we covered to the test. Below are some suggestions for how to improve your awareness of your nonverbal cues, as well as how you might try out and improve your openers.

Body Scan

Take a moment now to scan your body from head to toe. What do you notice about how you are sitting, standing, or lying? If someone walked by you right now, what do you think they would observe, without you saying a thing? Now, look around you. If there are others around, what do they seem to be telling you with their face, their stance, and their hands?

Through the Eyes of a Child

Have you ever noticed how children can watch television shows without any sound? Give this a try. Put on a random TV show that you haven't watched before and mute the sound. Without being able to hear the actors' words, pay attention to the way they look, their mannerisms, and what emotions they seem to display with their face.

Now answer these questions:

- *Whom do you find the most approachable and the easiest to start a conversation with? Why?*

- *Whom do you want to avoid at all costs? What led you to this conclusion?*

- *How well do the actors seem to communicate with one another? What are your clues?*

Mute the Media

Once a week, watch five to ten minutes of newscasts, TED talks, or YouTube videos with the sound off. Use it as a chance to remind yourself about the power of nonverbal communication and practice awareness of how our nonverbals shape our conversations.

Pair and Share

Ask your accountability buddy or another friend whom you trust to do a role-play with you. Practicing will help it feel less foreign and more natural when you embark on the real thing.

Follow these steps.

Part 1

1. Practice saying aloud your favorite openers to your buddy.

2. Share with your buddy what it was like for you to set the stage.

3. Ask your buddy what it was like to listen to your openers. Ask them for their feedback on your words, vocal quality, pacing, and nonverbal communication.

4. Improve the wording and delivery of the openers, based on the feedback you got. Write out the new wording in your journal.

Part 2

1. Think about the person you wanted to speak to when you identified your goals at the beginning of this book.

2. In a new role-play, pretend to be that person, so that you can experience what it's like to be in their shoes.

3. Ask your buddy to be you in the role-play and to verbalize your favorite openers.

4. Debrief after the role-play, considering how it feels to be on the receiving end of these openers.

5. Again, update and edit the openers as needed.

Part 3

1. With your twice-revised openers, practice setting the stage once more with your buddy.

2. This time, ask your buddy to pretend to be the person you are striving to speak to. If your buddy does not know this person, share a little bit about the person to help your buddy get into character.

3. Cue your buddy to honestly respond to the opener in the role-play.

4. Hearing your buddy's honest reply to your opener will give you further input on how your opener is coming across.

Timing Is Everything

When deciding to embark on a constructive conversation, ask yourself: *Is this a good time to do so? Am I in the right headspace to do this? How about the person I'm about to talk to?* In general, it's a good time to talk when you are well-rested and in a decent mood—and if the other person is too, even better!

Bad times to broach difficult topics include when you or the other person is hungry (low blood sugar can impact certain people significantly), has a headache, is tired, or especially if they're in the middle of a stressful life change like a breakup, new job, or loss of a loved one. Perhaps this should go without saying. But think back to some of your worst arguments—usually one or more of these conditions were present.

That said, we have both had effective conversations even when none of these criteria were met. The unfortunate reality is that many of us are walking around tired and stressed on a regular basis, and so you may decide to carry on with constructive conversations even when the timing isn't perfect. Because is there ever a perfect time?

Consider these questions, to help you decide for yourself if the timing is good, or good enough.

1. How much time do I have for this conversation? We recommend that you have at least thirty minutes to spare. Will it take that long? Maybe not. You may speak for ten minutes, but also want time for yourself to reflect on what happened. Will it take longer than thirty minutes? That can also happen. The key is that you give yourself enough time to be able to engage and have a little time afterward to decompress.

2. What is my readiness for this constructive conversation at this moment? If it doesn't go well, how will I take it? Am I prepared for an unsuccessful outcome? What am I doing after this conversation? If you have something high stakes happening later that day, you may find that embarking on a constructive conversation could zap your energy, distract

you from other tasks you need to attend to, or throw off your plans by consuming your thoughts and emotions. Talking to another person you trust, meditating, going for a walk, listening to music, or doing another kind of self-care activity are all great things to do after a constructive conversation. Remember the mason jar you made in Step 3? Go use it!

3. What state of mind does the other person appear to be in? Pay attention and observe the person you are about to speak with. What mood do they appear to be in? Do they seem tired or irritable? With someone you see regularly, you can always decide to embark on setting the stage at another time, when they are calm and well rested. With strangers or acquaintances, you may assess that it's a "now or never" situation. If you decide to proceed, be aware that their readiness and willingness to receive your message can be contingent on their mood and circumstances. Furthermore, you are not a mind reader—so in trying to decipher what mindset and mood the other person is in, you could be off.

Addressing these questions will help you gauge whether this is the proper time for yourself and the other person to set the stage. That said, it is also very important to note that one may never be truly ready to initiate or receive a constructive conversation. When it comes to having conversations about anything challenging, don't fall into the trap of never taking the plunge. While we do strongly encourage you to assess your readiness, do not take this as an opportunity to delay the conversation forever. Because you know it will be difficult, you might find yourself coming up with all kinds of "it's not a good time" excuses. So be aware. Don't use bad timing as a perpetual excuse for not opening up the conversation.

If you find yourself putting off initiating conversations again and again, remember:

1. It's okay to be nervous and even to be afraid. Don't misinterpret nerves and trepidation as reasons not to act. Trying

anyway will decrease the anxiety and teach you that you can handle this.

2. Imperfect action is better than inaction. You might not use the perfect words, but that's perfectly okay.

3. Keeping quiet tends to preserve the status quo. Speaking up, in and of itself, can be powerful and inspirational.

Summary

You've started practicing one of the most challenging parts of the 8-step model. Learning how to set the stage involves actually uttering words to someone other than yourself, in a way that's mindful of the content and delivery of your message. You are opening the door for a constructive, collaborative, and genuine dialogue. Hopefully, you now feel more confident to verbalize an opener that is anchored in your values. You also have some tangible tools to help you set the stage with an intentional, well-timed approach.

But we're not done yet. More is around the corner. Productive, healing action is within your reach.

TAKE ACTION

This is the moment that you've been waiting for. Probably, when you picked up this book, it was because you wanted to take action and have a constructive conversation with a friend, coworker, or loved one about a pressing cultural issue. But as you've learned, the process begins with a lot of inner reflection (Steps 1–4). Now that you have a solid foundation, you're ready to launch into that much-anticipated constructive conversation!

In this step, we discuss the three critical ingredients to taking action. We provide illustrations utilizing these ingredients in various contexts and with various people to help you clearly communicate your goals and values—and in turn to hear the goals and values of your conversation partner. Knowing these ingredients and seeing how they come together in these examples will ensure that you are able to take action and move through the full Kim Constructive Conversations Model.

Essential Ingredients to Taking Action

No matter the context and the person with whom you will be speaking, there are three essential ingredients to ensure the success of any action: Why This Person(s), My Experience, and The Ask (abbreviated Why, Me, Ask).

Why This Person (Why)

The first essential ingredient involves clearly expressing *Why* you are broaching a conversation with this particular person(s). Quite simply, Why this person? This is an important factor in that it communicates and highlights the connection between those involved. This might be reflected in the nature of your relationship as well as the quality of that relationship.

Why is this important to stress? As you recall, the Kim Constructive Conversations Model places great emphasis on relationship connection as well as the possibility of healing. When we broach difficult topics, it is easy to forget or even neglect the connection (or the possibility of a new connection) between one another. If the connection is not acknowledged and nurtured from the outset, then the road ahead can quickly become a slippery slope.

All trained psychotherapists know that what matters most in any therapy is the therapeutic relationship. The research on this is robust and compelling as indicated by various reports from the American Psychological Association's task force on evidenced-based therapy relationship (Norcross and Lambert, 2018). This alliance is vital, as the client often shares difficult personal material, and as the therapist inquires and, at times, even therapeutically challenges, the client. What ultimately matters in the challenging but rewarding work of psychotherapy is indisputably the relationship. So, it's no surprise that underscoring the relationship for those having constructive conversations can make a huge difference. After all, the delicate and even polarizing social context against which constructive conversations take place can be viewed as the difficult history and challenges that a client and therapist must together face.

You will also notice that prioritizing the relationship in any constructive conversation very much aligns with the importance of values. For example, maybe the nature and quality of the connection between you and the other person is one that is reflected by love, gratitude, or respect—such might be the case with family members or close friends. By highlighting such positive values, you are better able to manage and even neutralize barriers, including fear of damaging the valued relationship.

Recall the case of Tim and Rose. As Tim takes action with Rose, his Why might be captured in this way: "Rose, I am reaching out to you because you are an esteemed colleague and I respect you very much."

My Experience (Me)

The second essential ingredient involves your specific experience—your thoughts, feelings, or concerns. What about your particular experience do you want to share with the other person? Maybe that their prejudicial behavior hurt you. Or how their notable silence, when you most needed an ally, made you both angry and sad. Or that their bigoted speech is simply not acceptable in your home.

The *Me* experience is hands down the most sensitive content you will be communicating. On its own, it definitely has the potential to not only sting, but also to trigger conflict or even more serious consequences. So yes, it can, and most likely will, feel intimidating and nerve-racking to share your truth with someone who does not already see it. But remember, you are buttressing this sensitive content with two other essential ingredients that will soften the blow and help maximize the other person's ability to hear and receive what you have to say.

In the case of Tim, this might be: "Rose, I am feeling quite confused and disappointed about your decision to reject the qualified Black applicant, especially since we were tasked with helping to diversify our staff."

The Ask (Ask)

The third and final essential ingredient in taking action is what you are asking or seeking from the other person—what is your *Ask*? Since it is a conversation and not a monologue you are attempting to have, you must clearly communicate what you are hoping to achieve by starting the conversation. You must offer an invitation to mutually engage.

Certainly there will be the pull to tell the person off, correct them, criticize them, teach them, and just be done after you've shared your piece. But remember, then it would not be a constructive conversation you would be having! Constructive conversations are indeed about sharing your experience—in a respectful manner that can be received and heard. It is also about listening sincerely as well as a deliberate intention to engage in mutual dialogue.

Going back once more to Tim, his Ask might be reflected in the following: "Rose, I would appreciate very much having an honest conversation with you about all of this. This is important to me. And I know it's important to you. I want to figure out how we can better understand each other and work this out."

Notice in Tim's Ask that he gives Rose the benefit of the doubt regarding the importance of her experience. Tim also asks to work together with Rose, thereby aligning himself with her. This is no easy task, especially when Tim feels that Rose is clearly in the wrong. However, Tim also knows that framing Rose as being "wrong" and himself as being "right" will not lead to anything constructive, and certainly not to a resolution. In fact, it would only increase tension, bad feelings, and even gridlock. As such, Tim thoughtfully crafts his Ask in a manner that is honest, emotionally responsive (versus reactive), consistent with his goals, and generous in assuming Rose's goodwill. This in turn maximizes the likelihood that Rose will both hear Tim out and respond favorably to his request to engage and work together.

The best kind of Ask is one that promotes responsiveness and mutuality. In general, we recommend that you give the other person the benefit of the doubt and an opportunity for them to save face, even if they are obviously in the wrong. We are not suggesting that you lie or dance around the truth. Rather, we encourage you to accentuate that which matters most in having a successful constructive conversation—a mutual openness and willingness to share honestly and listen deeply. This means that we consider others in the same manner we ourselves would want to be considered—with compassion and generosity. Recall the reality of imperfections we highlighted earlier in this book. We are all perfectly imperfect. As such, the more we can hold one another with grace and mercy, the greater the chances that we can heal together.

Does the Order Matter?

The order of the above essential ingredients is flexible. However, generally speaking, the order in which they were presented—Why, Me, Ask—would be ideal in most situations. Starting off by emphasizing the relationship connection communicates its importance. It also serves as the soft cushion onto which the more sensitive material can land. Sharing your experiences and perspectives can then be received with more support. Finally, clearly communicating the Ask—your wish for mutual engagement—will allow what you just shared to be viewed as not merely a standalone complaint or criticism. Rather, it has the potential to be received as something that the other person can possibly engage with and even influence (e.g., clarify a misunderstanding or apologize for an insensitive mistake). This, in turn, becomes a two-way street—where both can be mutually involved and impacted.

If another order works better for you, or different orders work better in different contexts with different people, by all means, go for it! The point is not to be rigid or apply a strict formula. Our intention is simply to provide you with clear but flexible guidance and rationales. It is ultimately your journey, so be curious. Try out new approaches. And don't be shy about making it your own!

Alicia's Turn

Last year, I attended a professional event and was feeling inspired and grateful toward the organizers. I publicly thanked them and shared with the audience that I was especially touched that two women of color were the leaders. My intentions were positive, but as I sat down after speaking, I realized that I might have misgendered one of the organizers I was speaking about.

I felt horrible. I debated whether I should just leave it alone or take action and approach the person I might have used the wrong pronoun and gender identity for. I really liked this person and definitely did not want to do something that hurt them. But I was also embarrassed, and it felt tempting to just avoid it all.

Ultimately, I gathered up my courage and asked the person if they had a minute. We sat down together, and I said something like, "I was so moved by all the work you put into this event that I wanted to recognize you and communicate this publicly. But now I'm afraid I may have misgendered you without realizing it. So I just wanted to check in with you about this, and I'm so sorry if I did." In this scenario, I took action by communicating how I respected my colleague [Why], sharing my feelings, offering an apology [Me], and checking in about how my colleague felt about things [Ask].

The person was very gracious. They said, "I feel comfortable being identified as a woman when it helps other women of color. I do prefer the 'they' pronoun and am in the process of being more open about this and letting others in my professional circle know about this. I appreciate you checking in."

I responded, "Yes, I wasn't sure if I should, but I'm glad I did too."

I felt nervous while taking action, but I pushed through despite my nervousness. It was brief but meaningful, and I have no regrets.

Your Turn

It's time to turn to your journal. Consider a recent difficult dialogue you had or a constructive conversation you would like to have in the near future. Once the details of this conversation are clear, answer the following questions.

- **Why This Person.** *What about this particular person and your relationship with them would you like to recognize and highlight? What is the nature of your relationship with them? Family member? Coworker? Friend? Stranger? How would you describe the quality of this* relationship? (Hint, think about your values!) Maybe a loving daughter? A coworker you respect? A loyal friend? In the case where you don't already have a relationship with the other person, such as a stranger, what relationship values would you like to help guide your exchange? Maybe a connection that is mutually respectful? One that assumes good intention in one another?

- **My Experience.** What about your specific experience, thoughts, and feelings do you want to share? Remember, this is a tough one. But it is possible to balance honesty and compassion. In fact, telling our truths and sharing them with others can be perceived as an act of kindness, respect, and faith. (There go those values again!) You love your mother enough to tell her your truth. You respect your colleague enough to tell him your truth. So, what is your truth that you would like to share?

- **The Ask.** Finally, what do you want from the other person? What is the Ask? An inherent assumption in the Kim Constructive Conversations Model is to mutually engage and maybe even heal. Again be reminded of your values. What values promote mutuality? With your personal values in mind, how you would like to ask and invite the other person into this space of connecting? Write it down.

Pair and Share

Now that you are getting the hang of the essentials in taking action, let's role-play a conversation to practice. You can practice with your accountability buddy or recruit someone else you trust. Or, if you don't have a role play partner, try to imagine both sides of the conversation on your own. This practice will help prepare you to be truly open to the thoughts and feelings of the other person, just as you are asking them to be with you.

Follow these steps that gradually build to the action step.

1. *Carve out thirty minutes for the constructive conversation—or practice conversation.* As we mentioned in Step 4, the amount of time needed varies, but we have found that thirty minutes tends to be sufficient time to be thoughtful, deliberate, and patient. Pick a time when you're rested and energized. If you're a morning person, consider choosing the thirty minutes after you eat breakfast. If you know you're too stressed during the week to even consider this, do it on the weekend. And of course, as much as possible, it would behoove you to also be mindful of your conversation partner's schedule and routines!

2. *Take three deep breaths.* With each breath you take, imagine that you are more and more ready to begin. With each exhale, let out the tension and stress that will get in the way of focusing on your goal.

3. *Observe the person you are about to speak with.* (While this step may be less relevant for the role-play, still practice asking the following questions because they will be helpful for the real thing.) Do they seem ready for this conversation? What barriers might be present for them? While you are not a mind reader, having some gauge of where the other person is in the moment can be helpful to know. You have been preparing for this moment, and they likely have not. If you suspect that they may be caught off guard, for example, then you might build in more patience for any shock or defensiveness they may react with. If you know that they are already irritable for some unrelated reason, consider rescheduling the conversation. Not only is this considerate, but it would also minimize unintentional barriers. Remember, the goal is to maximize your chances to be heard, to listen, and to engage mutually and meaningfully.

4. *Practice positive self-talk.* Say a few things to yourself to pump yourself up. Be your own cheerleader, and tell yourself, *I can do this, I'm ready for this moment, I've prepared and now is the time.* This is also a chance to remind yourself again of your values: *I have courage with me, I have nothing to fear, I am grateful to have this opportunity to talk about this, I will let love guide me.*

5. *Open up the conversation.* Choose and say one of your openers. In addition to your words, use body language that communicates openness. This might include smiling (or at least not frowning!) and facing the person you are talking to with an open stance (no crossed arms).

6. *Time to act.* Offer *Why* you have broached a conversation with this person. Share *your experience*—your thoughts, feelings, or concerns—and remain open to theirs. Finally, clearly communicate *your Ask*—invite them to engage.

Practicing in role-plays gets you ready for the real deal. As with learning a language, there's no way to become proficient except with practice. We have been complimented by colleagues and friends for having amazing delivery and word choice during tense moments, especially around cultural issues. We were not born with this talent—it is truly a skill that we have crafted and practiced over time.

That said, who you are talking to can dramatically impact how you proceed. Now let's see the different ways taking action can look, depending on who you are broaching.

Taking Action

The steps in this book will embolden you to have constructive conversations with anyone and everyone. However, the way you speak to various people—family members, friends, colleagues, acquaintances, and even strangers—can vary quite a bit, depending on their relationship with you. Similarly, the way you proceed with this process will likely depend on who you're speaking with.

Let's get you prepared to take action with a variety of different people in your life.

With Family Members

Speaking with family can be a tall order. Many of us have family members that we care about but with whom we disagree. Family members have a unique way of getting under our skin. Therefore, engaging in constructive conversations with family can be especially daunting and emotional for everyone involved. As illustrated above, reconnecting with the values that are most important to you, and possibly the values that are also important in your family, can help guide the actions you are taking.

Meet Anna and Her Parents: Constructive Conversations with Family

Anna is beyond excited that her long-time boyfriend Mohammed has just proposed. After relishing her new identity as a fiancée for a few minutes, she is eager to share the wonderful news with family and friends. Suddenly, her heart sinks at the prospect of speaking with her parents. Even though they have been restlessly waiting for her to get married, they are not exactly thrilled with Mohammed as her boyfriend, never mind her fiancée! In spite of their supposed open attitudes, they have always made it clear that Anna should marry someone who is culturally and religiously similar to her family. Let's see how Anna might broach a conversation with her parents about her recent engagement to Mohammed.

> Step 1—Goal. Because Anna deeply respects her parents, she wants to be honest with them and tell them directly and promptly about her engagement.

> Step 2—Barriers. This will not be easy. Anna is fearful about what will happen after she tells her parents. Anna wonders, *Will*

they reject me? Will they reject Mohammed? Will they attend the wedding? She is questioning whether she will be able to keep her composure, to remain respectful even, if her parents respond negatively. After all, this is her mom and dad, and she loves them very much. She also loves Mohammed, and wants more than anything to be his wife. The stakes are high.

Step 3—Values. Anna's chosen values include love, respect, and honesty. She loves her parents and truly appreciates how they have been there for her and sacrificed for her over the years. She does not see her decision to marry Mohammed as deliberate disrespect of her parents' wishes. However, she suspects that her parents will see her choice as a rejection of their values and Christian faith. With all these worries in mind, Anna takes a few deep breaths and grounds herself in love, respect, and honesty to have the confidence to proceed.

Step 4—Set the stage. Anna decides to go over to her parents' house on Sunday and attend church with them. After church, they will be going to brunch at one of their family's favorite spots. Anna decides that speaking to her parents after their meal will be a good way to broach the conversation. Anna recalls that in her childhood they would have "family meetings" as dinner wound up, and so she feels comfortable initiating this conversation in a similar way. When the time comes, Anna opens up to her parents in a steady voice, saying, "It is really important to me that I'm honest with you, and so I'm going to take a risk and share something new that's happened." While Anna has a tendency to cross her arms during hard conversations, she mindfully and purposely keeps her arms at her sides, so as not to be perceived as closed off to her parents.

Step 5—Action. As Anna transitions into taking action, she reaches over to hold her mom's hand, and says calmly, "Mom and dad, I love you both so much. So I wanted to share that Mohammed and I have decided to get married. I am so happy! He is such an important part of my life, and so are the both of you. Your opinion matters so much to me. So I want to keep the lines of communication open between us. How are you feeling about this news?"

Notice that when Anna takes action she expresses *why* she is broaching a conversation with her parents—because she loves and respects them and they are important to her. Her values of love, respect, and honesty are evident. She then shares *her experience*—her happiness to be engaged to Mohammed. Finally, *her Ask*—to invite her parents to share their thoughts and feelings about the news she just shared. As you can see, each part of Anna's action has meaning and intention. Furthermore, the delivery factors we covered in Step 4—vocal quality, volume, and pace; nonverbal communication; timing—all matter here as well.

How Anna's parents ultimately respond is not fully within Anna's control. However, as demonstrated in the steps above, Anna did everything in her power to help maximize her parents' responsiveness to both her news and her wish to engage mutually, respectfully, and constructively.

Words for Action

Here are some examples of specific ways to phrase taking action with different family members.

PARENTS AND ELDERS

Our parents seem to irritate us in ways others can't, even if they tried. So talking to moms, dads, and those who have raised us is especially hard. Grandparents' opinions and judgments can have a particularly biting quality. Rather than shrug the issues off to generational differences alone, try talking to them about it.

We hope these sample phrases of taking action can help you get the job done.

- "You are such an important person in my life, and I look up to you so much. [Why] Because I respect you, I wanted to be honest and share that when you use racial slurs to refer to certain people of color, it feels very hurtful. [Me] I know you don't mean any ill will, but it definitely bothers me a great deal. It would mean a lot to me if we could talk about this. [Ask]"

- "I'm proud to be your daughter. [Why] It's hard for me, though, when I hear you say things about women that I find demeaning. [Me] Maybe I am misunderstanding your intentions. If you are open to it, I would love to talk more with you about this. [Ask]"

- "I'm feeling uncertain about how to point this out, because I respect you so much. [Why] When you told my girlfriend and me that 'marriage should only be between a man and a woman'—this really hurt me. [Me] I know you love me but I'm confused about why you said this when you must realize that, as a lesbian couple, a statement like that would hurt us. Can you help me understand where you were coming from? [Ask]"

CHILDREN

On the other end, children can be notorious for not wanting to talk or listen to their parents. So for you parents out there, try these on for size.

- "As your parent, I love you so much and I am here for you. [Why] When you said 'that's so gay,' I was taken aback because I want you to respect all people, regardless of who they like or love. [Me] I assume you probably didn't mean anything by it, but that expression is very hurtful and demeaning to a lot of people. Can we talk about it? [Ask]"

- "Hey son, I heard from your teacher that someone made fun of your name today. [Me] How are you feeling about it? [Ask] I want you to know that I'm always here for you—to listen to you and to protect and help you whenever you need. [Why] (*Notice how the order here is Me–Ask–Why. A good reminder that order is flexible and should be based on your personal preference and the situation at hand.)*

SPOUSES AND PARTNERS

Communication in intimate relationships and long-term commitments is crucial. Any bad communication habits we have with those we date or have partnered with will often carry over to the constructive conversations we attempt. Do not let this dissuade you! Instead, try to draw on the positive communication habits that you've developed over the course of your relationship and remember that your significant other is worth the effort.

- "We've been together for a while, and our relationship means so much to me. [Why] I know sometimes I avoid talking about issues that I think will lead to an argument. But one topic about our son has been on my mind a lot lately, and I want to talk to you about it. I want to support John in painting his nails and wearing the clothes he feels most comfortable in. [Me] I know you have strong feelings about this. I know you don't want him to wear 'girly' things. But I think it's really important for us to find a way to support John. Can we try to figure this out together? [Ask]"

- "I want to understand why you always say something disparaging about people who are homeless when we pass them on the streets. [Ask] It makes me wince every time I hear you mutter something disrespectful under your breath. [Me] I love you and respect you very much [Why], so this part of you makes me totally confused." (*Here the order is Ask–Me–Why. Mixing it up can work.*)

EXTENDED FAMILY

With family we don't see as often, it can be tempting to avoid constructive conversations altogether, especially if we only see them during holiday get-togethers. Sometimes adult siblings, cousins, aunts, uncles, and other extended family members fall into this category. Even though conversations with distant relatives can be especially challenging, taking action with extended family can still be worth it!

- "We don't see eye to eye on immigration, and it feels like the elephant in the room that we are always avoiding. [Me] We are family and we care about each other. So I really think we can talk about this. [Why] My goal is not for us to change each other's minds. I would love it, though, if we can respectfully hear each other out. Maybe afterward we could simply enjoy fellowship with one another without feeling like we're walking on eggshells. [Ask]" (*Here is yet another different sequence to the order.*)

- "You have always had a special place in my heart. I also know how intelligent you are, and I greatly respect your ideas and beliefs. [Why] However, I'm totally baffled about your decision to not support a great political leader just because he made some silly comments about women many years ago. [Me] Instead of bad-mouthing each other in private, I am hoping we can be brave and have an open and honest discussion about this. [Ask]"

CLOSE FRIENDS

How does that saying go? "You can choose your friends but you can't choose your family." So what does that mean for constructive conversations? Choose to have them!

- "If you are willing, I would appreciate an opportunity to revisit and maybe even deepen our conversation from yesterday. [Ask] There is something that rubbed me the wrong way [Me], and I wanted to let you know and talk about it openly because I value our friendship. [Why]"

- "Our friendship means the world to me. [Why] So it's hard for me to express this, and yet I also want you to know that I was really upset when you told me my boyfriend wasn't good enough for me because he 'only' graduated from high school [Me]. It seems like your perspective comes from a place of love for me. I want to understand more about what you're thinking and feeling. [Ask]"

As we mentioned before, the order of Why–Me–Ask is flexible and interchangeable. Our individual styles and even cultural backgrounds will influence which order feels most natural for us. So take the creative liberty to borrow the examples we've provided that you like, throw away the ones you don't, and of course come up with your own.

Your Turn

Let's work with the expression "family first." So, applying this saying, prioritize front and center having hard but important conversations with your family. Who in your family do you want to speak with? What about? Now turn to your journal and write out your plan for Steps 1 through 5 for this family member. Take the time to write these steps out as clearly as possible, similar to how we did for Anna. Once you've completed this in your journal, if you feel up for it, schedule a time to have this conversation with your family member.

At Work

Just as families tend to have their own dynamics that make direct communication challenging, places of work also have their own nuances, complexities, cultures, and expected codes of conduct. There are a myriad of ways that your workplace might not feel conducive for taking action. And there may also be certain aspects that make it feasible to take action sometimes, with some people, in some spaces.

CASE STUDY

Consider the following work scenario. An agenda item at the meeting includes the annual mandatory diversity training for all staff members. The only Black woman at the meeting, Valene, proceeds to draw from her own personal experience at the firm, and describes it as an isolating place at times. Another colleague, Jennifer, a white woman, explains that she disagrees with the mandatory nature of the training and questions its utility. Jennifer expresses her concern that there seems to be an over focus on race, at the expense of other important issues. Kevin is the facilitator of the meeting. See below how he proceeds and applies the steps.

Step 1—Goals. Kevin's goals include facilitating a successful meeting, in which those in attendance feel like the agenda items were covered and everyone had a chance to be listened to and heard.

Step 2—Barriers. Kevin identifies the following barriers: Relatively new to the company, he is unsure how others perceive him and how they feel about him. This uncertainty contributes to Kevin feeling unsure about himself, which can negatively impact his ability to take charge and speak his mind.

Step 3—Values. Kevin values bravery, strength, and teamwork. He sees these values as worth living up to, even when his confidence is low and he is faced with challenges.

Step 4—Set the stage. Kevin observes, "I noticed that the mood in the room has changed. While it may be difficult to talk about, I do want us to return back to the agenda item of annual diversity programming."

Step 5—Action. "We've heard some important perspectives already. Thank you. I hope that as colleagues we can be open and respectful with one another as we share our thoughts and experiences about these important issues. So, let's spend a bit more time on this." Depending on who speaks next or if no one speaks, additional action follow-ups Kevin can take may be "I'd love to hear from those who haven't had a chance to share yet" or "I really want to empathize with Valene's feelings of isolation. What can we do as a firm to make our place of work more inclusive?" or "I understand how difficult talking about this issue can be. Being relatively new to this company, I'm trying to figure out what I think and feel about this idea as well. I also believe that if we speak up and engage, we'll all be stronger as a team because of it."

Can you identify Kevin's Why–Me–Ask in his action statements?

WORDS FOR ACTION

Each organization, whether it's the food business, retail industry, or corporate settings, has its own set of work values and norms that might make constructive conversations less or more inviting. Furthermore, the power dynamics in work settings add complexity to effective ways of taking action. Below are some ways to verbalize taking action with different members in the workplace.

WITH YOUR BOSS

There is typically a hierarchal structure with management and employees that significantly influences what can and cannot be said. An employee may understandably be concerned and wonder, *If I take action, what will happen? Will this impact my annual review? Will this jeopardize moving up in the company?* If you find yourself in this scenario, the following approaches for taking action might be a good fit.

- "I've been thinking about the discussion we had yesterday during our weekly meeting. There is something you said that I didn't quite understand. [Me] I wanted to follow up because I am invested in our work and professional relationship. [Why] When might be a good time for us to connect? [Ask]"

- "I disagree with the decision you made today. [Me] I respect your leadership and know you have in mind what's best for the company. [Why] So, I was hoping you could expand on your thought process a bit more as to why you made that call. I also hope I can share some of my own ideas for possible solutions. [Ask]"

WITH YOUR EMPLOYEE

Managers and supervisors may have their own questions: *If I bring this up, will this person view me differently? Will this hurt productivity? Will this stir the pot?* However a manager decides to proceed, here's one action approach that might be useful.

- "I value you and your contributions to this company, so I wanted to come speak with you directly [Why]. I received feedback that you said some things during staff meeting that were concerning. [Me] I wanted to hear your perspective and experience of what happened. I also want to speak openly and directly with you about these claims. I hope you'll consider having an honest conversation with me. [Ask]"

WITH YOUR COWORKER

Colleague-to-colleague is another type of relationship, which may make taking action feel threatening. Since many people spend a large amount of time in their workplace, coworkers often become a social group, a source of belonging and community. So if you take action with a coworker, you may worry about what might happen if things go awry. Common concerns may include, *Will I no longer have a lunch buddy? Will other colleagues judge my actions, or gossip about me?* Here are some examples of taking action with a coworker that might apply to you.

- "The collegiality we have in our lab is amazing. I am grateful we are team members, and I trust that we can talk through any issues [Why]. In that spirit, I'd love to speak with you about something important. [Ask] I overheard you talking about one of our coworker's physical appearance. What I heard made me feel uncomfortable. I am not sure what you meant by it, so I wanted to check in directly about it with you [Me]."

- "I always look forward to your light-hearted jokes at work—you help all of us get through what is usually a very long day! [Why] But when I heard you make a disrespectful joke about the only person of color in our office, I was honestly quite shocked and speechless. [Me] I know you and I know you didn't mean any harm, but I wanted to talk with you about why I found the joke so offensive. I would also love to hear about where you were coming from. [Ask]"

Many people spend more time at work than at home, and so it makes sense to prepare ourselves for having such constructive conversations about culture in the workplace. While it can get complex and tricky with the power dynamics present in a place of work, we still think it is possible to have these conversations effectively. In fact, we would argue that in order to have inclusive and healthy workplaces, it is paramount to have such conversations.

In the Classroom

As professors of psychology, we regularly collect written feedback from students during the middle of a term to see how the class is going. One year, a couple of students in Alicia's class anonymously expressed great concern that the three men in a class of twenty were dominating class discussions, speaking first and taking up more airtime.

Alicia's goal was to create a classroom culture that was multiculturally affirmative. Grounded in the values of integrity and diversity, she worked through her external barrier of limited class time and the risk of negative student course evaluations, and her internal barrier of self-doubt. In this circumstance, taking action involved updating the entire class about this feedback and opening up space to discuss this matter. Specifically, Alicia set the stage by saying, "I've received some important feedback from a couple of you, and I'd like to carve out some time to share this with the group and also discuss together. While it changes the plan for today as listed on the syllabus, I think it's a change worth making."

Transitioning into taking action, Alicia said, "Creating an academic community that is inclusive is an important part of learning. In the midcourse feedback, a couple of you shared that you are feeling demoralized by the group dynamics. More specifically, it was noted that there are concerns about the way that the male students take up a lot of space in the class by tending to speak first and for longer periods of time. I also have noticed this pattern and would like to open up a discussion to see how others are feeling about it." Alicia then attempted to broach the issue at hand in a direct way, while also inviting discourse. By carrying through with this action, Alicia generated a class culture that promoted open discussion and communication.

In this scenario, the initiation of a constructive conversation also opened up paths for addressing gender norms and speaking about the ways they influence group dynamics. Role-modeling a constructive conversation for a group you are leading paves the way and gives permission for others in the group to continue having these conversations in other settings.

If Alicia hadn't taken action, resentment in the class could have grown, the learning environment might have become tainted, and the students who bravely shared the feedback may have felt further silenced, while the male students in the class would have been left unaware of the impact they'd had on others.

Your Turn

What cultural dynamics are present in your place of work or school that you want to address? What inequities or injustices need to be talked about? Gender gaps? Lack of diverse representation? Now is the time to plan out your action step. Write out the questions and observations you want to verbalize. Next, schedule a time you will broach these issues. Thinking about these ideas is fruitful—we also want you to go out and put them into practice!

With Strangers

With family, friends, and workmates, the decision to pursue a constructive conversation can come from a desire to engage more authentically with someone you care about or someone you see on a regular basis. This is typically not the case with a stranger. So why take action with strangers? Who cares? You'll never see them again, right?

Even so, there may be times when you do decide that it is meaningful to engage in a constructive conversation with a stranger. The reasons we commonly see for taking action with strangers include protecting one's integrity, standing up for what you believe in, and speaking up for someone or a group of people you care about.

In these scenarios, you may find yourself thinking, *If I don't say something now, how will this person ever know it bothered me? If I don't act, I'm just part of the problem.* Those that identify as allies to marginalized communities will often find themselves in these situations.

Other times, with strangers you might decide to confront the person, express your anger, maybe even tell them off, and then walk away. For too long, marginalized communities have been silenced by others or forced to silence themselves. And so there may be times when speaking your mind forcefully and loudly is appropriate, deserved, and needed. We are not advocating for dehumanizing the person you are confronting, nor are we advocating violence. Not at all! However, we must acknowledge that there are times you will want to engage in a constructive conversation, and other times that you won't have the energy, time, will, or desire. There are times in life when people, especially those with marginalized identities, need to and should speak their truth, in the moment. And that can be healing too.

Engaging in constructive conversations with strangers tends to be driven by a desire to right a wrong, stand up for a principle, and raise new ideas with new people. At times, it can be less about the other person—you don't exactly know them well, after all, and so it's often more about you and your identity.

CASE STUDY

Consider our earlier case of Elizabeth. She decides to take action and speak with Manuel because she is proud of her wife and their son and does not want to hide.

Elizabeth broaches a conversation with Manuel and says, "You are kind to compliment my son. [Why] My wife and I are indeed very proud of Jason. I want you to know that Jason has two moms that love and raise him. When you assume a dad is in the picture, it feels invalidating to me. I understand that may not be your intention, and so I hope it's okay that I shared this with you. [Me] I'm also open to hearing any thoughts you have about what I just shared. [Ask]"

Note that Elizabeth, in this process, opens herself up to possibly hearing a response that she finds hurtful and invalidating. For those who do want to broach constructive conversations with a stranger or an acquaintance, here are some ideas around phrasing:

- "While we belong to different political parties, we are both Americans. So, from one American to another [Why], I hope we can respectfully hear each other out [Ask]. I imagine that what you just said was not intended to be offensive, but for me, it was really hard to hear. [Me]"

- "I overheard you making a comment about people who are Muslim. What I thought I heard you say, I found to be hurtful. [Me] Because we are neighbors and I respect how kind you have been to me and my family over the years [Why], I would like to get together some time to clarify any misunderstandings. [Ask]"

- "I know we don't know each other very well, but I feel connected to you through the church we both attend. [Why] I'd like to take a risk and tell you about some concerns I have about [insert topic here]. [Me] I'd really appreciate your help in better understanding your perspective. [Ask]"

CASE STUDY

When exiting a plane, Jeff notices Ava, who is walking with a probing cane and appears to be blind. Ava is speaking with two airline attendants. As Jeff watches, the male attendant tries to escort Ava into a wheelchair and help her by taking her bags without her permission.

Initially, Ava tries to inform the attendant that she did not request the wheelchair. The attendant appears to be confused and insists on the wheelchair. Ava then becomes angry and raises her voice, expressing that she's not being heard.

Jeff is torn. He wants to step in and advocate for Ava, but he also does not want to suggest or imply that Ava can't handle this situation on her own. Jeff is aware that his getting involved could come across as an able-bodied man jumping in to "save" a woman with a disability. Jeff doesn't want any actions he takes to be condescending, sexist, or ableist. Jeff has a friend with cerebral palsy who uses a wheelchair and often talks about her struggles with different airlines, and so Jeff feels a personal connection to Ava's situation as well.

Before taking action, Jeff integrates a check-in when beginning to set the stage. Jeff says to Ava, "Excuse me, it's hard for me to stand back and not say something here when it looks like you are not being listened to. I also don't want to overstep. I am happy to get involved if I can be of any assistance."

Jeff then listens to Ava to see if she does indeed want help and is okay with him stepping in. When given the green light, Jeff proceeds to take action by saying to the airline attendant, "Excuse me, sir, it seems like you are trying to help, which is great. [Why] However, I'm noticing that there may be some serious miscommunication here. It sounds like your customer is letting you know that she does not need assistance, and yet I'm hearing you insist that help is needed. As a fellow customer, I am concerned about the way this is being handled. [Me] Is there some airline policy you are required to enforce that we are unaware of? [Ask]"

Jeff's words give some in-the-moment feedback. He anchors himself in the shared role of customer to connect with Ava in an egalitarian way, voice his concerns, and take action as a bystander ally. He also connects with the airline attendant, to whom Jeff's action is targeted. He is careful to give the attendant the benefit of the doubt instead of outwardly chastising him. What values do you think might be reflected in Jeff's action?

This example shows how you can take action with a stranger when the topic at hand involves someone else. Speaking with strangers presents unique dynamics because there is no preexisting relationship to base the conversation on.

Since you lack information about the person you're about to talk to, be prepared for a range of possible responses, from openness and apologies to anger and lashing out. If, for whatever reason, you are concerned about your physical safety, we strongly encourage you to pause before acting. For example, let's say you are in a taxi very late at night in an unfamiliar city you are visiting. The driver says something culturally offensive. You consider initiating a constructive conversation, but you realize if the driver is not receptive to the conversation, many things could go astray. What if the driver abruptly ends the ride and you are stranded? What if the driver becomes angry and their driving ability becomes impacted? This is a scenario in which some might opt against moving forward with a constructive conversation.

If possible, another option is to call or text that buddy of yours to get their perspective on the situation before acting.

Your Turn

What issues have you encountered with strangers that you'd like to address next time it happens? Adolescents using homophobic language? Older adults being talked down to? Identifying the issues now will get you prepared to speak up, offer that comment, or pose that question next time it occurs.

In preparation for that future constructive conversation, write out your Steps 1 through 5, do a role-play to practice, and then go out there and start the conversation.

Now that you've read through ways to take action with family, coworkers, and strangers, we'd like you to reflect further in your journal.

Consider taking the thirty-day challenge. For thirty days, challenge yourself to have constructive conversations around every microaggression and macroaggression you experience firsthand or witness. Do the thirty-day challenge with a buddy or group of people. Then you can discuss and debrief about the conversations you have along the way.

Summary

Taking action puts it all out there. You might be making an observation, giving feedback, and asking a question. Whatever format your action takes, please remember the three essential ingredients that will help ensure the success of your action: highlight your connection with other person, share your specific experience and perspective, and communicate your Ask—the wish to engage and dialogue. And as always, hold on to your values: the key to navigating these uncharted territories.

As you anticipate the countless ways taking action can transpire, you can become familiar with how taking action might differ based on who you are speaking with and under what contexts. Remembering your values and practicing and preparing for taking action are ways to help ground you so that you can take a stand when the time comes.

LISTEN

Congratulations on making it this far! You're doing great. But don't get too comfortable. We're not finished quite yet. You have now entered the realm of listening, which comes with its own host of challenges. But don't fret. In this step, you will learn not only to effectively manage common pitfalls but also to maximize your listening skills, moving you even closer to completing a successful constructive conversation.

Your Turn

Before we dive in, let's take a quick inventory of your listening skills. Having a good sense of your personal baseline for listening will help you understand your areas of strength as well as areas for growth. It will also help you figure out where you should invest your energy.

Grab your journal, and write down the answers to the following questions.

1. Rate your overall listening skills.

1	2	3	4	5
Nonexistent	Poor	Okay	Good	Excellent

How do others describe your listening skills? For example, have you ever been told you are a good listener? How often are you the person to whom family and friends reach out to during challenging times? How often have others broached constructive conversations with you? Do you recall how you listened then?

2. Think about the last time you experienced a difficult interpersonal exchange. Maybe a time when you shared something difficult with someone you care deeply about, or a time when it was challenging to listen and hear someone else tell you something uncomfortable, or a time when a minor misunderstanding led to a big conflict. Which of the following roles did listening play at the time? Jot down all that apply.

    - *To fish for a specific response (for example, an apology)*
    - *To learn something new*
    - *To prove your point or argument*
    - *To judge, criticize, find flaws*
    - *To find common ground or connection*
    - *Other reasons*

    Some of these reasons, intended or not, can make the task of listening, and ultimately constructive conversations, more challenging. Others can make them easier. Consider which ones support listening, and which do not.

3. What factors facilitate your listening ability during difficult interpersonal exchanges?

4. What factors get in the way of your ability to listen during difficult interpersonal exchanges?

Effective Listening

Now that you have some sense of your baseline listening skills, let's get right to it. Listening is absolutely critical to communication. But most of us, truth be told, are not that great at it. In fact, many of us tend to overestimate our listening skills. This is true even for those whose profession is all about listening. Humbling, isn't it?

So, no matter who you are, every one of us can benefit from strengthening our listening skills. It can't hurt and it will most certainly help with your constructive conversations.

In case you're wondering if there are right and wrong ways to listen—yes, there are! To help you figure this out, here are some do's and don'ts for effective listening.

Do:

- Give your full, undivided attention. You had your turn—it's now the other person's turn. So close your mouth, open your ears, and give your full, complete, and undivided attention to the speaker.

- Maintain eye contact. This is simple. It is also the single clearest nonverbal way of showing the speaker that they have your attention.

  Note: Having said this, we acknowledge that like many behaviors, eye contact is culturally bound. The right amount and intensity of eye contact depends on the cultural background of the person you're speaking with. Whereas the mainstream American culture generally values direct eye contact, in other cultures this might symbolize disrespect. So be mindful of the cultural congruence between you and the other person.

- Turn your body toward and slightly lean in to the other person. Creating this intimate physical space will communicate interest. It will also allow you to pay better attention.

  Note: Like eye contact, physical space between people is also culturally determined. The right amount of personal space for one person might not be the same as it is for another. The person on the receiving end might feel that you are encroaching on their personal space—or that you're not close enough! As before, be mindful and attempt to assess whether you and the other person are operating from similar or different cultural expectations.

- Check your face and body language. We communicate with our face and body just as much as we do with spoken words. This is especially true when we are listening—since we're being quiet, our facial expressions and body language can shift into high gear. Consider some common nonverbals, discussed in Step 5.

  Note: Again, there is great variability in nonverbal communication across cultures. But it's helpful to remember that if our nonverbal cues are inconsistent with our verbal language and intentions, they can thwart our best communication efforts.

- Offer an occasional uh-huh or a nod to convey that you are listening and tracking what the other person is saying.

- Minimize distractions. When we're emotionally activated, it can be hard to resist distractions. Intense emotions often bring discomfort, and we are socially conditioned to avoid or repel what's uncomfortable. Because this pull is so strong, we have to actively resist it. For example, if your cell phone rings while the other person is talking, don't answer it! Better yet, make sure it's turned off before you even get started.

Don't:

- Speak—it's not your turn.

- Interrupt. This might seem obvious, but it can be difficult in practice. Interrupting includes finishing the other person's sentence or talking over them before they are done. We suggest you also hold off on any clarifying questions, as these too are disruptive to the speaker. Be patient. Who knows, the clarification you seek might be the next thing the speaker says. If you find not interrupting challenging, imagine placing an invisible tape over your lips to keep them closed. Or literally bite down on your tongue (gently) as a reminder to not speak.

Note: We acknowledge that interruptions during conversations is more common among some cultures, families, and even individuals. Do your best to practice what you believe to be appropriate, and remember that it might be interpreted differently than you intended if the other person is operating from a different set of rules.

Your Turn

Practice makes perfect! The next time you find yourself listening to someone, practice these suggestions. This is an exercise in giving your full, undivided attention. If you can, plan to do it every day. The more the better! Ask someone an open-ended question, and practice—maybe ask your child about their day at school or your coworker about their weekend. It can be brief, just a few minutes even. You can do it anywhere—at work, school, on the bus, at the supermarket.

As you get better at it, up the ante. Ask questions on topics that are sensitive or controversial. Maybe even pose questions to someone who you know holds very different opinions from you. Are you still able to give that person your full, undivided attention? You don't have to agree or become their BFF. Instead, you are strengthening an important skill that will undoubtedly keep you firmly on the path to having constructive conversations.

Anatasia's Turn

Nonverbals are challenging for me. I come from a very expressive culture and family. We talk voluminously with our faces and bodies. Indeed, it's a very important part of how I communicate with my family and community.

For as long as I can remember, I've been advised and even instructed to "fix" my face, that is, be more neutral and less expressive. Coming from family or close friends, this was one thing, but when such suggestions came from other people outside my circle, it held an entirely different meaning. It often meant someone in a position of power and privilege didn't understand or like what I was expressing nonverbally. My nonverbals were also interpreted against the stereotype of the demure, quiet, deferential, and submissive Asian woman. (There are no such women in my family!) So, what I heard was this: "Be more like me"; "I don't like that you are different"; "You can't look at me like that—do you know who I am?" As I felt invalidated and subordinated, my nonverbals would shift into overdrive. This, in turn, usually resulted in more misunderstanding, conflict, and disconnection.

It's not uncommon for people with marginalized identities to be told to make themselves more palatable to those with privilege. This includes facial expressions and body language. Let us be very clear—this is *not* what we are asking you to do. In fact, the burden of making your nonverbals more palatable to others, especially those who hold power and privilege, is not yours to bear. Instead, it is symptomatic of oppression itself.

It is also true that people with marginalized identities often adjust their natural nonverbals in order to fit in, be accepted, be hired or not fired, and simply survive. For some, this happens outside their conscious awareness and is deeply internalized. For others, code-switching occurs intentionally: smiling, nodding, and quieting body gestures to appear nonthreatening. The alternative may pose risks to their safety, acceptance, access, and love.

We encourage everyone, regardless of identity, to challenge the status quo. If you are bold enough to attempt constructive conversations, try to be strong enough to resist social conditioning. This involves challenging your proclivities and judgments as they arise. If you are a person of privilege (white, male, affluent, straight, able-bodied), resist the pull to ask a person with a marginalized identity to adjust their nonverbals to be more agreeable with you. This might be as simple as wondering about the quality of their eye contact or the position of their bodies, or analyzing their expressions. Instead, consider the possibility that your interpretations of the other person's nonverbals might be entirely subjective, inaccurate, and even oppressive. Even if you don't believe you are doing this, remind yourself that you have been socialized to do so. Socialization is not your fault, but it is your responsibility to do something about it. Ultimately, it is the obligation of those who hold privilege to ensure that they are not unintentionally asking someone to edit themselves in order to feel more comfortable.

If you are someone with a marginalized identity, resist the pull to fix these things. This might be harder than you think, as you have been socialized to wear a mask, to make others feel more comfortable at your expense. It is not possible to connect honestly, with the intention of having constructive conversations, if you don't show your true colors. This does not mean, however, that you should go to the other extreme. To use an analogy, we are not suggesting that you show up in your figurative PJs, teeth unbrushed and dried drool on your chin. Put on your real face and show up dressed—not in some uniform someone told you to put on but in the colors and style that reflect who you really are. You are now ready.

Your Turn

How do you check your face and body language? That's right: practice. Yes, you can practice getting to know what your face and body are communicating nonverbally, with or without your knowing it. The more aware and in control you are of all the ways you communicate, the greater your chances of having a constructive conversation.

Here are some suggestions for how you can get started.

- *Review a video of yourself. Any recording will do. Turn the volume off and play the recording in silence. "Read" your nonverbal language. What is your face communicating? Your eyes, brows, the curvature of your mouth, and so forth? What about your body posture? Arms, hands, stance, and so forth? How about any physical* gestures? Get to know your nonverbal self. Do this with as many videos as you have access to and are able to review. The more you know about you, the better your chances of communication success.

- Solicit your partner, a family member, or a friend and ask them to have a conversation with you on a topic you feel passionate about. If you and your partner share different opinions, even better. Record the exchange, making sure you remain quiet while you listen to your partner share their thoughts on the issue. Act as you usually would. Then review the recording. What did your nonverbal language communicate? Did it facilitate or deter the quality of listening? Ask your partner about their experience and "read" of your nonverbal communication. Did your nonverbal language make your partner feel more or less heard?

- Turn to a news anchor, commentator, or personality you often disagree with. Record yourself watching a segment of their show. The more disagreeable you find the content of the show, the better. Now review the tape of yourself. What is your nonverbal language saying? Maybe your head is shaking, your lips pursed tightly, your gaze narrow or seething? Or maybe the corners of your mouth are turned down, or your eyes are rolling in disbelief? It might surprise you to discover that even against a computer or TV screen, your nonverbals are speaking back loudly.

Listening Accurately

Notice the speaker's word choices, which may differ from your own. As you listen, you might unintentionally translate their words into your own vocabulary—perhaps words that better suit your position or argument. This happens all the time. In fact, we often hear what we want to hear, instead of what was actually spoken. In low-stakes situations, this is not a big deal. *Tomayto, tomahto.* However, when emotions are running high and sensitive issues are involved, it can make a world of difference.

Ultimately, you want to connect honestly with the other person. After all, isn't that what constructive conversations are all about? To be brave enough to be honest. In order to be honest, you have to be true to the other person, including accurately acknowledging their word choices.

Be on the lookout. Make sure you code and store into your memory the speaker's actual words, not your translation of them. Listening accurately communicates respect and honesty to the speaker. This, in turn, will increase your chances of having a successful constructive conversation.

How to practice listening accurately:

- Channel your inner stenographer. Imagine you are a court stenographer, recording everything with meticulous precision. The expectation here is not for you to be perfect. However, remember that most of us overestimate our listening skills. We often end up hearing only a fraction of what was said, with limited accuracy. So channel your inner stenographer—a professionally trained listener—and see how much your listening accuracy improves.

- Quiet your personal translator. Don't allow your emotional filter to manipulate the speaker's actual words. Hands down, this might be the most difficult task of listening during constructive conversations. When your personal translator (perhaps in the form of emotional reactions) tries to interject and offer their own interpretations, politely but firmly insist you don't need their help. Even though it might feel good in the moment to corroborate your argument or position, remember that in the long run this only serves to get in the way of your constructive conversation.

If you are like some people, your inner personal translator might respond with, "See, I knew he wouldn't see it my way." Or maybe, "I don't think this is going to go well. Better throw in the towel before it gets too ugly." Or even, "Uh-oh, I think I offended them. I knew I should've just kept quiet." Although there might be some truth to these interpretations, they are more likely to derail, instead of support, the unfolding constructive conversation. So, politely thank them for their feedback and remind them that the most important task now is to listen, genuinely, and without internal interference.

Anatasia's Turn

Like many women in my family, within me lives a feisty, hot-tempered personal translator. Whenever there is any inkling of feeling challenged or disrespected, this translator comes out, arms swinging. In her full glory, her unsolicited translation usually goes something like this: "What?! Did you hear what she just said?? Are you gonna just sit there and let her talk to you like that?" The majority of the time, this hotshot translator has an important point to communicate. However, she unnecessarily elevates my agitation so that it's easier to react emotionally and harder to respond thoughtfully. Thankfully, over the years and with the use of the 8-step model, my personal translator has simmered down a great deal. She still pops up once in a while, uninvited, but when she does, her reactions are quickly calmed by the wisdom of my values, which help me to listen more fully with minimal interference. If I can do it, you can too!

Your Turn

Hopefully, it's clear by now that listening is no easy matter. Yet it's fundamental and critical to communication.

So, we encourage you to practice, practice, practice. You don't need a constructive conversation situation to improve your skills. Here are some ways you can immediately work on strengthening your listening accuracy.

- *Next time you are in a conversation with someone, listen with the goal of hearing accurately. Maybe as your spouse tells you about her frustrating day at work. Or your coworker explains their recent sales presentation. Or the man sitting next you to on the bus talks about the latest in local politics. How carefully did you listen? Do you remember what they said, in their own words?*

- *Turn back to that news anchor, commentator, or personality you disagree with. Listen again to a segment of their show. Maybe they are reporting or talking about immigration, climate change, health care, or standing for the anthem during a football game. Now pause your screen. Jot down what you think you heard the person say. Then rewind and play the segment again. How accurate were you? Did you change any of their words? The goal here is not to recall every single pronoun or preposition. Rather, did you listen carefully, making sure to honestly report what was said without interference from your personal translator?*

Listening for Intention

Have you ever been in a situation where you were trying to be earnest but your words or actions landed in all the wrong ways? Maybe you mistakenly assumed someone was pregnant and asked when her baby is due? Or at a funeral service, in spite of your best intentions to comfort the family of the deceased, you fumbled your words and instead made some silly comment about the hors d'oeuvre? Or maybe with your friend, who just found out that his partner had been unfaithful, in your attempt to console him you instead commented on his bad choices in men? In all these situations, the sting of your words is undeniable. However, if the person on the receiving end can see and acknowledge your good intentions, then your mistakes can be corrected and the relationship rupture mended.

In multicultural training, there's a common concept of emphasizing impact over intention. This is because, frequently, the person who perpetrates a microaggression claims some version of "that's not what I meant" and either refuses to or has a difficult time taking responsibility for the impact of their words or actions.

Without a doubt, acknowledging and being accountable to the impact of what one says and does is critical. This does not mean, however, that intention does not matter. Intention matters a lot. Often, when we are grappling with conversations on topics that are taboo, our expressed words or emotions might not match our underlying intentions or experiences. Our word choices or actions may be clumsy, awkward, and sometimes just plain wrong—which should come as no surprise. It's gonna be messy. This much we should expect. And the hurtful impact of someone's words or actions does not get a pass. Not at all. But we shouldn't turn a blind eye to their intention either. A person's intention tells us they are trying, and that matters. A lot.

Listening for intention is not as difficult as you might think. Here are some questions to help you easily identify someone's intentions.

- What is the other person *trying* to say (versus actually saying)?

- If I assume they have a good or positive intention, what might that be? What is the probability that this is true?

- If I assume they have a bad or negative intention, what might that be? What is the probability this is true?

- What am I focusing on? A few off-putting words? My emotional reactions to those words? What is the bigger picture?

- What is the underlying emotion of what the other person is saying? Maybe fear, anxiety, anger, regret, embarrassment, shame? Use this information to give yourself clues about where they might be coming from.

Your Turn

Listening for intention is a skill you can immediately start practicing. Here are some suggestions you might try.

- *Become a mediator. A low-stakes way to start practicing uncovering intentions is by helping others in distress. Maybe it's an argument between your children, coworkers, or friends. In helping someone resolve an interpersonal conflict, you can use the questions listed above to uncover each person's underlying intentions. Not surprisingly, you may get some pushback, as one or both people will no doubt ruminate on the verbal content. Your job is to both acknowledge the actual words and help the other person realize the intentions behind those words. How does bringing intentions to the foreground change the interpersonal dynamic and outcome?*

- *Recall a recent disagreement or argument you had with a friend or family member. Regardless of your feelings about the event, focus on the other person. What were they trying to say or do? In spite of what they actually said and how they said it, what do you believe was their underlying intention? Maybe in the heat of the moment, all you experienced was their inability or unwillingness to support you, and now, as you consider their intentions, you can see how they were, in fact, attempting to be helpful—or at least did not have bad intent? This underlying intention may have been obscured by your sole focus on what you perceived as unsupportive counterarguments.*

If you'd like to take this exercise up a notch, connect again with your friend or family member. Share with them what you believe was their intention. Were you right? How does acknowledging their intention impact your connection?

No Buts About It

As you listen, acknowledge internally, but table, any *rebuttals or counterarguments* that may develop. Wanting to defend your points and push back on anything you disagree with is completely understandable. But this is not the time or place. If you are preoccupied with preparing a rebuttal, it's impossible to give your full, undivided attention to what the other person is saying.

Of course, who among us have not been guilty of this at one point or another? We get it. This is not easy. In fact, tabling rebuttals might even feel downright aversive for some of you. Maybe even a sign of defeat. After all, we live in a culture of "don't let anyone push you around" and "don't go down without a fight."

But just because something makes sense or even feels good, that doesn't mean it will serve your goal. Remember, constructive conversation is not a tit for tat. You may certainly disagree and have different points of view and experiences, but ultimately constructive conversations are an attempt to repair and heal.

For those who have been subjugated for their identities, the strong pull to immediately correct inaccuracies or challenge oppressive assumptions is completely understandable. However, if you act on this pull before the other person has finished their sharing, it might jeopardize your ability to have the kind of constructive conversation you intended.

In spite of that, if what you are hearing is fundamentally disrespectful or threatening, you should take steps to care for yourself. This might mean disengaging as quickly as you can from the interaction.

Constructive conversations are not about diminishing and further oppressing those who are already disenfranchised. Such a dynamic is not healthy, and it would not constitute a constructive conversation. The same goes for anyone on the receiving end of any abusive exchange, no matter your identity. In situations like this, you must realize that a constructive conversation is not possible in this situation. At a minimum, it's not the right time. So please take care of yourself.

(Note: Discomfort from a difficult conversation is not synonymous with denigration of someone's identity. This is an especially important matter to consider for those who hold privilege.)

So, how do you quiet your rebuttals and listen with full capacity? Here are some suggestions.

- As rebuttals start to develop, consciously put them aside. Tell yourself: *I will get to you in due time; It's not my turn yet; Don't worry, you will have plenty of time to think, process, and speak.*

- Remind yourself: It's normal to feel defensive and to want to protect your perspective. However, you don't have to act on these feelings. Your experiences are no less true if you don't, and you need not feel threatened just because someone else feels differently.

- Bring your focus back to the speaker. Again and again. In attending to them fully, you ultimately enhance your own impact.

- Be on the lookout for *but I don't want to forget what I want to say in response!* When this happens, make a quick mental note and get back to listening. Trust that you will remember, especially if it's important enough. Constructive conversation is not a debate match with winners and losers. Content matters, but not as much as connecting sincerely and generously.

- Stay grounded in your goals. Hold onto the bigger picture—to repair and heal.

- How do *you* want to be listened to? With full, undivided attention? Or with attention that's compromised by the rebuttals the person listening to you is preparing? Extend the same courtesy you expect for yourself to the other person.

- Go back to those values! Respect. Integrity. Generosity. Compassion. Equanimity.

Your Turn

Let's put all of this to test. There's no better way to improve your understanding of something than by trying it out for yourself. Here are some ways you can do just that.

- *Go back once more to that news anchor, commentator, or personality you are unfavorable toward. Listen to a segment of their show—ideally something you have not previously viewed, so that the content is new and requires your full attention. The more you disagree with the person's views, the more challenging this exercise will be, so pick the segment accordingly. As you listen, notice if any rebuttals begin to form. If so, utilize the suggestions listed above to guide yourself back to attending to the show fully. Repeat this as many times as you need to. It may take a few tries. Be patient. When you are successful, move on to another segment by the same or a different commentator. Repeat this exercise as many times as needed until you begin to notice improvements in your ability. Ideally, practice as often as you can, across multiple days or weeks.*

- *Practice in your real world. Invite opportunities that present themselves to you in your daily life to practice listening without interference from rebuttals. Maybe over lunch with a colleague, discussing a conflict at work. Or with your spouse, about whether or not to purchase something that might exceed the family budget. How does listening fully influence how you are listened to when it's your turn? How does it impact the interpersonal dynamic or outcome? You may still disagree with the other person, but you may find yourself able to engage with more mutual respect and depth than you thought possible.*

Anchor in Your Values and Goals

Bring those values back! In addition to building your listening skills, based on the suggestions above, don't forget that values can and should be with you at all times. They will help to anchor you so that you can calmly, intentionally, and confidently practice all the skills you have learned.

Allowing your values to guide you throughout the journey will ensure that you remain rooted in your goals. If they are not already on your personal list, the values of patience and self-control may support you in the listening step.

Avoiding Common Pitfalls

In addition to the do's and don'ts, keep in mind some predictable pitfalls you must overcome if you are to successfully navigate the task of listening.

"I can't handle it—I'm out"

To start, you might have a difficult time settling down emotionally. Maybe the rush of adrenaline from taking action was more intense than you imagined? Maybe it triggered some unresolved or ongoing challenges? Or maybe the speaker's response to your action really got under your skin? In any or all of these cases, you might find yourself ready to walk away and leave—or at the very least, mentally check out. In your distressed state, you may begin to wonder why this was a good idea and question your ability and desire to move forward.

In the scenario with Anna, upon sharing with her parents the news about her engagement to Mohammed, she continues to experience a racing heart and nausea. In these moments after taking action, Anna is reminded of all the times in the past that her parents disapproved of her choices in dating culturally different partners. In addition to her initial anxiety and angst, she is now experiencing a growing sense of frustration, anger, and resentment. She suddenly feels less motivated to stay put and hear her parents out. In her activated state, she finds herself on the verge of yelling at them, as she has fantasized many times before. She begins to question whether she can actually handle the situation. Would it be rude to just get up and leave?

Imagine you are Anna. What would you do? Stay? Leave? Why? If you choose to stay, how do you imagine handling your emotional distress?

"I feel better! I'm done"

Another common pitfall involves the opposite scenario. You might find that you feel much better after taking action. You were able to get something important and burdensome off your chest, and eagerly welcome the new sense of levity. In fact, you begin to wonder if you really need to complete the remaining steps. I mean c'mon, why risk ruining your good mood, right?

Going back to Anna, instead of experiencing anxiety and anger, she might feel proud of herself for telling her parents so soon after Mohammed's proposal. She is fully aware she dropped a major bomb on her parents, and they will certainly feel some kind of way about it. But she doesn't want to compromise her high spirits. After all, wasn't the whole point to feel better about herself? Again, she considers leaving the restaurant, this time to protect and sustain her good mood.

Put yourself again in Anna's shoes. You can sympathize with her desire to preserve her good mood. At last, she did it. She stood up for herself and shared her good news, all the while knowing her parents would not be happy. What would you do? Would you leave the restaurant before giving your parents the chance to respond? Why or why not? If you choose to stay and risk compromising your good mood, what makes you do so?

"I'd better brace myself"

Often, when we are about to receive information that we might disagree with or negative emotions, we prepare ourselves, perhaps unconsciously, to reject it immediately. In other words, we brace ourselves, to ensure that nothing penetrates or challenges our beliefs or experiences. Of course, this is no way to listen.

In some cases, putting up one's guard has been a coping mechanism for surviving marginalization and oppression. As such, it can be viewed as self-protection and a means of preserving one's fundamental worth and truth.

Unfortunately, such a response can also contribute to unintended negative outcomes. These might include interpersonal disconnections, limits to understanding ourselves and others, and inevitable magnification of our collective pain. Ultimately, the answer to our suffering is not perpetually closing off and distancing ourselves from one another—in spite of the pain that we may have experienced and continue to endure. In the short run, disassociation might afford much-welcomed relief. In the long run, however, it serves only to exacerbate our pain and deepen our division.

For Anna, this might mean that even before her parents have a chance to participate in the dialogue, she has already written them off. Based on her past negative experiences, Anna braces herself for the worst. In fact, in her mind she is already planning her wedding without her parents, even pondering explanations she can give to the guests about her parents' absence on one of the most important days of her life. She convinces herself that nothing they say or do will ruin her wedding, not if she can help it.

Anna's reaction is understandable. She has reasons to believe that her parents will not respond favorably. But in bracing herself and in turn closing them off, how does Anna unintentionally sabotage her own goals? How might she instead acknowledge the sensitive history with her parents *and* also give them the opportunity to fully engage with her? After all, isn't this why she is attempting a constructive conversation? To connect differently in spite of what might have occurred in the past?

"Retreat! Abort mission"

Yet another common pitfall happens when we judge a book by its cover. As soon as you take action, and even before the other person has had a chance to utter a single word, you are immediately on the hunt for any signs or reasons to retreat and abort the mission. For example, you might read too much into the other person's facial reaction in search of clues that they will respond badly. Maybe it's the furrow of their eyebrows, the enlargement of their eyes, or their tightly pursed lips? No unequivocal evidence is required—just the slightest suggestion of a negative reaction is all you need to justify your decision to back out.

In so doing, however, you not only walk away from your goal, you also convince yourself that no good will come out of your efforts. Better to not waste any more time or energy.

In the case of Anna, this might play out in the heavy silence that quickly falls after she shares her news. Even though Anna doesn't know exactly what her parents are thinking, she reads too much into her dad's suddenly expressionless face, as well as the deep flush of rising emotion on her mom's cheeks. Anna interprets all of this as proof that no matter how hard she tries to listen, it's useless to attempt a constructive conversation with her parents. So she might as well stop here. No need to wait for her parents' verbal response. Their protracted silence and the look on their faces say it all.

From Anna's perspective, would you come to a similar conclusion, based on her parents' nonverbal language? What might be some additional interpretations that would allow you to stay and give them the chance to offer their full response? What would it take to shift this uncomfortable dynamic into a mutual and reciprocal dialogue?

"The hard part is over"

A final common pitfall involves a deluded sense that the hard work is now behind you. Since you courageously waded through your personal barriers, fought back the ghosts of your Pandora's box, and mustered the strength needed to speak your truth, you figure the hard part is over. Therefore, you assume that all will be smooth sailing moving forward. Cruise control, here you come! For the time being, this pitfall keeps you in the game. However, given your investment in this illusion, it will only be a matter of time before the desire to bail quickly comes into play.

Let's go back once more to Anna. After relaying the news of her engagement to a man her parents disapprove of, Anna is feeling a huge sense of relief. She made it! Instead of hiding the news or even eloping without her parents' knowledge (which she seriously considered), Anna was able to broach her parents and speak her truth. In spite of knowing that her parents' reactions will be anything but congratulatory, she believes that what lies ahead cannot be as bad as making the first move, right?

Given Anna's belief that the hard part is behind her, what do you anticipate she might encounter as this scenario with her parents unfolds? How might she feel good about her accomplishments thus far *and* also maintain realistic expectations as she moves forward?

Managing Pitfalls

Taken together, all the pitfalls we just discussed have one thing in common: self-preservation. For each of the pitfalls, there is a hidden desire to protect oneself from possible rejection, loss of control, and pain. As such, fear and anxiety take over and our primal fight-or-flight instinct gets activated, and our automatic aversion to discomfort makes the choice of flight very tempting. The prospect of "fight," on the other hand, might raise more angst. So how do you stay and continue to engage (e.g., fight) when the impulse to flee takes over? Here are some recommendations.

- **Acknowledge and normalize your experience.** Listening well does not mean abandoning your own experience. Quite the contrary. In fact, in order to listen fully, you first need to acknowledge what is going on for you. This does not mean you shift attention away from the speaker onto yourself. Rather, as you notice your own feelings, thoughts, and reactions, understand that they are normal. You can simply be aware of these experiences as they arise. And you can, just as simply, set them aside for when it is your turn.

You can practice acknowledging and normalizing your experience by adopting the "both/and" approach. You can both have a lot going on within *and* create room to listen to someone else.

Remind yourself: *This is normal. I don't need to figure it all out now. I can and will attend to my thoughts, feelings, and reactions later, when it's my turn. For now, it's important that I pay full attention to ensure the best chance of having a constructive conversation.*

Breathe, look inward, acknowledge, reassure, and turn to the task of listening.

- **Get up close and vulnerable.** Moving closer to the person may not feel like the obvious solution, especially if you're feeling the impulse to flee. Yet it's one of the most powerful tools to bring about change and healing. Of course, getting intimate requires tremendous vulnerability, something that makes many of us a bit uneasy. This is particularly true when sensitive and controversial topics are involved. However, in order to fully absorb, process, and be impacted by what another person has to offer, we must have the courage to be vulnerable.

  Vulnerability is, in fact, one of the most underutilized interpersonal tools. In many cultures, we have been socialized to believe that vulnerability is a sign of weakness. Paradoxically, it is the one emotion that affords the greatest likelihood for relationship connection, as well as for healing. Think about those feel-good movies where, at the end of the film, the protagonist finally professes their love to someone, offers a much-anticipated apology, seeks forgiveness, or makes the ultimate sacrifice in the name of justice. The vulnerability projected in these stories can become so contagious that it makes us, as audience members, feel just as good as the actors we are watching. Who knows, it may even lead us to act more kindly to our own family, friends, and strangers.

Why? Because vulnerability draws people in and is able to effectively abate difficult emotions such as anger, guilt, blame, and shame. We respond to it by softening, remaining open, and feeling inclined to share our own vulnerability. All of this is magic for relationship connection.

You can practice vulnerability, quite simply, by listening with your heart. More often than not, in difficult dialogues we listen with our critical brains, through the lens of our past wounds, and guided by a personal agenda. This yields a specific outcome—greater interpersonal distance. By contrast, practicing vulnerability means listening with a full and open heart. This means you have to be willing to receive, acknowledge, believe, and be impacted by whatever may come. Grounding in values of love and kindness would certainly help here.

This is definitely a big ask. But big efforts yield big payoffs.

Your Turn

Bring out your journal. Now, imagine a constructive conversation you hope to have one day soon. Based on this scenario, answer the following questions. Consider this as a part of your planning for the future constructive conversation.

1. Imagine your future constructive conversation, in which you just took action. Now take careful inventory of how you are feeling.

2. What are the bodily sensations you anticipate you might be experiencing?

3. What are the emotions you anticipate you might be feeling?

4. What are the thoughts you anticipate you might be thinking?

5. Knowing yourself, what are some pitfalls that you suspect you might encounter? Think vividly and honestly. Write down how the scenario would most likely unfold—the more details the better.

6. How might you respond to your anticipated pitfalls? How would you remind yourself that what you are experiencing is normal and to be expected? How can you remember your goals and values? To stay put and move forward? Write a brief memo to yourself. Give yourself a pep talk. Address all the excuses and "yeah, buts" that might tempt you to reverse course.

Summary

We covered a lot of ground in this step, probably more than you expected. So, here are the big takeaways.

Listening is a complex, multilayered experience. It requires that you engage fully, accurately, and with minimal distractions and interferences. It involves concerted effort to uncover the speaker's underlying intentions and to attend to your nonverbal communication. It also mandates identifying and managing common pitfalls, which, if you're not careful, could derail your intentions.

In order to listen deeply and meaningfully, you need to get up close. To do so, anchor again in your values. Allow your values—maybe those of courage, compassion, patience, and faith—to help keep your heart open, your ears curious, and your connection to your goal unobstructed.

Finally, don't forget to be brave enough to be vulnerable and be affected. This will most certainly lead you to deeper relationships with others and, ultimately, closer to constructive conversations.

RESPOND

It is now time to respond. As you may have already guessed, there's more to this than meets the eye. But don't fret. We have solid suggestions to support you, including tips on how you can avoid common pitfalls when responding. We got you!

You are so close to having the full constructive conversation experience. You can do this!

First Response

Responding is a critical process that can deepen the quality of a constructive conversation or kill it dead in its tracks. Here are some suggestions to guide you through your process of responding.

Ground into Your Values

First and foremost, you have to ground. This should be quite familiar by now. Ideally, you have been practicing and strengthening this skill of grounding throughout the earlier steps (see Step 1 if you want to review).

This is a time when you will be tempted to react impulsively instead of responding thoughtfully. So, pause for a moment and take a deep breath, collect your thoughts, and soothe your emotions. Tell yourself, *I can do this. It's not easy, but I am brave. And I will stay true to my goals and intentions.* Remind yourself that you've come a long way already through the preceding steps and likely much farther than you've traveled before. You don't want to veer off course now.

So, get quiet and go back to your values. They will again be your anchors, keeping you grounded and aligned with your intentions. Don't be shy—use them liberally! Dig deeper into your commitment and hold onto them firmly—they will continue to guide you through. Maybe the values of patience, faith, and compassion can support you here.

Your Turn

You don't have to wait for a constructive conversation to practice responding skills. Here are some common day-to-day situations to help you further build your skills. Feel free to brainstorm other daily stressors that you may encounter on a regular basis. (There are plenty to choose from in our fast-paced and stress-inducing world!) These can be mild to moderate in intensity; they don't have to be anything super serious. The idea is to give yourself ample opportunities to practice.

Practice your grounding skills in the following situations:

- *Someone cuts you off while driving.*

- *Your child throws a tantrum.*

- *Someone at work (client, boss, co-worker) speaks to you disrespectfully.*

- *Your date or friend is running very late (again) for dinner.*

- *Your cousin sends you an unexpected email criticizing your behavior at the last family gathering.*

- *Any other situations that come to mind.*

Anatasia's Turn

Throughout my life, I have heard many variations on the proverbial phrase "When life gives you lemons, make lemonade." In the face of adversities, small and large, my parents, teachers, and other elders encouraged me to respond with optimism and a can-do attitude.

To a child who was seldom happy-go-lucky, this was a tall order. My baseline fluctuated somewhere between moderately annoyed and perennially cranky. Rare was the picture of me as a smiling teenager. So the idea of responding to life's lemons by making a delicious glass of lemonade did not (and still does not) come naturally or easily. Instead, my instinct was often to throw those lemons back, saying, "No thank you! And you better not throw them again!" Though immediately gratifying, this move predictably did not yield many lasting benefits.

As I got older, I realized the importance of consequences and outcomes. Of keeping my eyes on the prize and not sweating the small stuff. However, I also noticed stark differences that could not be ignored or justified. For example, I saw that not everyone had to contend with lemons. In fact, some had never had a lemon before, only lemonade. Then there were those who bore their inequitable share of lemons, often through no fault of their own. For these folks, no matter how much they struggled, they had little power and influence to stop the lemons. Injustice was clear.

But what to do? I knew I had to do more than just throw those lemons back. It became clear that I had to work with others—with those who had lemons as well as those who didn't—in order to make the best lemonade for all. (And I would be lying if I didn't admit that at times I still have to resist the impulse to throw back those lemons.)

I share all this to say that responding with grace can be incredibly challenging. Like you, I am still humbly learning, practicing, and growing. To this day, before responding to something sour that someone has said, I have to remind myself to stay focused on my goals, which are always bigger and more important than any one lemon, no matter how large or sour. I push myself to keep returning to my values of hope and, yes, even a can-do attitude. And I remind myself that success in life is ultimately about one's commitment and resolve to do things others are unable or unwilling to do.

So, if you're like me—a temperamentally cranky kid in a grown-up's body, fantasizing about hurling lemons—I empathize. I know this step of responding will not be effortless. But know that you are not alone. We are in it together. Now, let's make some lemonade!

Appreciate the Speaker

Depending on what you just heard in Step 6, you might be thinking, *Are you kidding? You want me to thank them for sharing? Did you hear what they just said?!* Okay. Pause, breathe, and ground. Yes, bring those values back. In fact, keep them nearby at all times.

We agree that even the mere suggestion of appreciating the other person, especially if they just shared something triggering or provocative, may not be the first thing that comes to mind. We get it. But hear us out.

Recall that the other person probably did not have a chance to prepare before being solicited for a difficult dialogue. Most likely, they are not operating with a preplanned goal or even tools to help manage their reactions. It would be safe to assume that this is not easy for them. In fact, one may argue that the whole experience may be harder for them than it is for you. After all, they were the ones pulled into an unanticipated situation. In spite of this, they stayed, listened to you, and offered their perspective. They engaged.

Remember that productive engagement is what we are striving for. So don't get side tracked by the imperfections of what was said. Imperfections are to be expected. So are strong feelings from everyone involved. Use your values, and hold on to the bigger picture: your goals.

So, yes, no matter what the other person said (unless it was threatening or abusive), some form of appreciation is warranted. You are thanking them, not for the content of their words necessarily but instead for their willingness to accept your invitation and engage with you in this challenging endeavor. Be the bigger person that you are fully capable of being. Not only is this the respectable thing to do, it will also start you off on the right foot as you respond.

In the case of Tim, upon hearing Rose's defensive response to his comment about the importance of prioritizing staff diversity, he could say, "Thank you for your willingness to have a conversation with me about this. I know it's not easy to talk about." Or "I really appreciate the chance to have an honest conversation with you about this. I know this is not easy for either of us." Guided by his values of gratitude and compassion, Tim is genuinely able to appreciate Rose. This, in turn, will set the stage for Rose to be more responsive to whatever Tim will say next.

Your Turn

You can start practicing this appreciation skill right away. How? Immediately bring "thank you" back into your life in a big way. Everything we need to know, we really did learn in kindergarten! Saying "thank you" and "please" absolutely matters. These small but important gestures most definitely create positive connections in relationships. So use them—for everything that feels appropriate and even for things that might feel like a stretch.

For example, if your coworker asks whether you will be going to the staff meeting, say, "Thanks for asking—yes, I will be there." When your waiter refills your water, say, "Thank you." If your date calls to say they are running late again, say, "Thanks for calling to let me know." (You can be annoyed and still appreciate that they at least called!) When your child whines that they don't like what you cooked for dinner, say, "Thank you for letting me know." (You can convey that their opinions will be heard and still expect them to finish their dinner.) Finally, include "thank you" and "please" in electronic communications (text, email, social media). Yes, we live in a culture that expects, even demands, shorthand and brevity. However, you can also agree that much intimacy is lost in connecting this way, regardless of how efficient it might be. Some things just can't be rushed. So take your time and go the extra mile. A little appreciation goes a long way.

Don't forget your values! They are the pillars of this model. Anchor yourself firmly in them. Values of gratitude and compassion might resonate here. Gratitude can help you have sincere appreciation for the other person's engagement—they didn't have to stay, but they did. Compassion can help you realize that this is not easy for them either. Aligning with your values will again keep you steadfast as you move through this important step.

Acknowledge What Was Said

In this stage, you're simply letting the other person know that you did in fact hear what they said. If you just received an earful of insolent comments, this might feel challenging. Still, you can do this!

Hopefully you were using your listening skills from Step 6. In addition to the full, undivided attention you gave the other person, ideally you also listened for accuracy and intention, set aside any rebuttals, and anchored your listening in your values. Maybe the value of honesty encourages you to acknowledge the veracity of what the speaker said? Maybe the value of courage allows you to validate their words, in spite of their uncomfortable impact on you? Again, allow your indispensable values to shepherd you when emotional storms threaten to take over.

When acknowledging the other person's sharing, try to:

1. Start with your intent to acknowledge (e.g., "I heard you say…," "If I understood you correctly…," "It sounds like you…").

2. Aim to accurately identify the person's:

   a. Intention (e.g., to correct your misunderstanding of them, resolve past conflict, defend their experience, or better understand you).

   b. Content—what they actually said. And whenever possible, include their specific word choices in your acknowledgment.

   c. Accompanying emotions (e.g., angry, remorseful, defensive, or surprised).

3. Invite any corrections about the accuracy of what you heard or interpreted. A checkout can often accomplish this, such as "Did I hear you correctly?" or "Did I get that right?"

In the case with Tim, he might say, "Rose, what I heard you say was you believe that hiring the Black applicant over the white applicant would be a 'form of racism.' And this frustrates you very much. In fact, you wish the company would not engage in 'reverse discrimination.' Did I understand you correctly?"

Your Turn

Using the three suggestions above, practice the acknowledging skill as much as you can in various settings with different people.

For example, in the above scenario with the child whining about dinner, you might acknowledge the child in this way: "Thank you for letting me know. It sounds like you don't like the vegetable stir-fry. You know you should eat vegetables because they are good for you. But you're mad because there is so much broccoli, which is the 'worst food in the whole world.' Is that right?" (Yes, this might sound a bit awkward or silly. But stick with it. You are practicing an important skill. In time, you will find your own unique words and voice.) With this response, you appreciated your child's engagement, conveyed that their opinion matters, and that you respect them enough to listen to them accurately. If you still expect them to eat their vegetables (including the broccoli), the fact that you respectfully listened and responded to your child will undoubtedly yield a better outcome and connection than if you responded reactively.

Maybe your values of gratitude and compassion can again guide you here. Compassion will remind you that your child is still young and attempting to navigate their ability to express their preferences and assert their will. You will remember that this is normal (it's easy to forget, especially when you're tired and your child's tantrum is unrelenting). Gratitude will help you appreciate the fact that your child feels safe with you to express their feelings, even when they don't agree or are upset. Allow your values to again be in the driver's seat. They won't steer you astray.

Share the Impact

Understandably, you might feel compelled to respond quickly and reactively—to correct the speaker, argue back, or even put them in their place. Although some of these options might feel good in the moment, they would ultimately jeopardize rather than enhance the constructive conversation.

But make no mistake. By no stretch of the imagination are we implying that you should stay quiet. Not at all. Your response, specifically the *impact* of what the other person said, most definitely matters and should be shared.

Impact is related to but not the same as what you might reactively say or do. For example, your initial reaction might be one of anger and indignation—the full impact, however, is likely not captured in this immediate reaction. The true impact of what the other person said lies further beneath the surface. It reflects your deeper, more vulnerable experiences and feelings. Maybe underneath the initial anger is pain? Fear? Sadness? More than the actual words spoken by the other person, impact reflects the *meaning* those words had for you. It captures the profound truth of your experience.

It is, however, more difficult to access and infinitely more challenging to share. Why? Because it requires that you be open and vulnerable to your deeper experience. As we discussed in Step 6, for most of us vulnerability can be scary.

Using courage to unlock and practice our vulnerability can be the single most powerful tool we can use to stay connected with others. So we challenge you to be brave enough to be vulnerable. When this happens, not only do you help disarm the defenses of the other person but you also enhance the likelihood of being heard.

In the case of Tim and Rose, driven by his anger, Tim considers ripping apart every inaccuracy in Rose's response. This includes the fact that the two candidates were equally qualified, and that Tim and Rose were tasked with the goal of helping to increase staff diversity. However, if Tim is able to pause, breathe, and ground into his values of courage and vulnerability, he can instead share with Rose the impact of her words. He could say, "Rose, I'm feeling quite confused and a bit hurt. I respect you very much. So to hear that you don't support prioritizing diversity and inclusion in our company feels surprising and personally very disappointing."

In sharing your impact, here are a few do's and don'ts to keep in mind.

Do:

- Use "I" statements.

- Share your vulnerable feelings. This will help the other person stay open and more responsive to what you are about to say.

- Look for and highlight relationship connectors—actions that help to build positive connections in the relationship. For example, to a family member you are having the constructive conversation with, you might say, "In spite of our differences, I know we love one another. Otherwise, we wouldn't care so much about each other's opinions and feelings."

Don't:

- Use "You made me feel" or "It's because of you" statements (e.g., "I was minding my own business, then you criticized me for no reason, and now I'm very upset.").

- Only share your reactive feelings, often anger or outrage (e.g., "You don't know what you're talking about."). This will close off and shut down the other person to what you are about to say.

- Reject, discredit, or invalidate the speaker's response. These are relationship interrupters—actions that disrupt or erode connections in the relationship (for example, Tim to Rose, "You are totally off base. You have no idea why this is important, do you?").

Your Turn

You can immediately start practicing and building your impact-assessment skills. Here are some suggestions to help you get started:

- *The next time you receive any negative comment or feedback, assess and communicate the impact it had on you.*

For example, if your partner makes an unfavorable comment about a new purchase you just made, suppress the impulse to immediately and defensively lash out (e.g., "I bought it with my own money, thank you!" "What about what you just bought the other day?!" "I didn't ask for your opinion or permission."). Instead, ask yourself what effect his unfavorable comment had on you. What feelings lie beneath your angry reaction? Maybe hurt, insecurity, or disappointment? Whatever it is, share that with your partner (e.g., "Ouch, that hurt"; "I feel self-conscious when I'm criticized"; "I thought you'd like my new purchase. I'm disappointed that you don't approve.").

- *In addition to actual experiences, you can also reflect on past events to grow your skills in uncovering impact.*

  For example, what was really going on with you when you had that heated exchange with your friend about immigration reform? Maybe you were hurt that your friend shut you down before you could fully share your thoughts? When you were told you were "wrong," you immediately became angry and lashed out. But upon reflection, you realize you were hurt because you thought you had a strong enough bond to have an open and honest disagreement with your friend.

- *As always, use values to practice your grounding skills and remain aligned with your goals.*

Hope for the Future

An added bonus to any response should include a sense of hope. This is essentially the wish you have to move forward together. Despite your potential desire for a definitive resolution, final steps to constructive conversations are few and far between. In fact, we caution you to be wary of happy endings and foolproof solutions after just one encounter.

This does not mean that a singular constructive conversation cannot have vast and lasting impact. Certainly that is possible. But it would be naive to assume that all challenges have been resolved and no more work is required after just one conversation. After all, the goal isn't about crossing some imaginary finish line. Rather, it is to stay engaged courageously as long as possible and as long as it takes. To that end, hope is critical.

More likely than not, upon parting, you will each be walking away with more questions, concerns, or unsettled feelings than before you started. But don't be discouraged! This actually means something important has been stirred and transformation may be underway. As such, the ending, for now, will almost always close with "to be continued." In conveying your hope as part of your response, you are acknowledging the need and wish for more engagement.

In the scenario with Tim, he might relay to Rose, "I want very much to better understand your perspective and see if we can figure this out. Maybe we can grab coffee before our next meeting?" You can see how Tim anchors himself in the value of hope and possibly faith: hope that his continued engagement and commitment to working with Rose will result in a favorable hiring outcome, and faith that their relationship is strong enough to endure and even thrive after more conversations.

Your Turn

Here are some suggestions for how you might include hope when responding to someone. Try them in your regular interactions—maybe at work with your boss, at home with your roommate, or in your romantic relationship.

- *"I really hope we can continue this conversation another time."*

- *"Maybe we can grab coffee next Friday to continue where we left off."*

- *"This was hard, but I think we are getting somewhere. I'd love to continue our talk to see where this could go."*

- *"I think this conversation is too important for us to stop here. I hope we can do this again soon."*

Putting It All Together: The Full Response

Here are some examples of how you might put all of the above suggestions together into an integrated, full response.

Tim and Rose

"Rose, thank you for your willingness to have a conversation with me about this. I know it's not easy to talk about. [Appreciate] What I heard you say was that you believe that hiring the Black applicant over the white applicant would be a 'form of racism.' And this frustrates you very much. In fact, you wish the company would not engage in 'reverse discrimination.' Did I understand you correctly? [Acknowledge] Rose, I'm feeling quite confused and a bit hurt. I respect you very much. So to hear that you don't support prioritizing diversity and inclusion in our company feels surprising and personally very disappointing. [Impact] I want very much to better understand your perspective and see if we can figure this out. Maybe we can grab coffee before our next meeting? [Hope]"

Other Examples

"Thank you for sharing your thoughts with me. [Appreciate] It sounds like, from your perspective, I misunderstood your intentions. Please let me know if I am off base. [Acknowledge] For me, what I thought I heard you say was very painful, especially given my personal experiences. [Impact] I hope we can continue to talk further about this, as it is important to me and I value our connection. [Hope]"

"Thank you for your willingness to talk with me about this. [Appreciate] I heard you say that my comments and actions were very offensive to you. Did I get that right? [Acknowledge] I was not aware of this. In fact, I was shocked to hear you say that my behavior had such a negative impact on you. I'm anxious to admit that I'm still not sure I fully understand. [Impact] However, because this is clearly important, I would like to take time to think more about what you just shared. I hope we can connect again to better understand each other and to clarify any further misunderstandings. [Hope]"

If it's helpful, use these as templates to practice and build your skills. As you become more familiar with the script, your own unique style and words will take hold.

Your Turn

Turn to your personal journal. Imagine the constructive conversation you hope to have soon. In this scenario, you have just taken action, received a response from the other person, and are getting ready to respond. For each of the questions, write down your answers.

1. Your first task is to *ground*. How do you visualize yourself doing this? Is there something you say to yourself? Maybe you breathe mindfully, to settle your body? What values can help guide you here?

2. Now you are ready to speak. First line of business: *appreciate* the other person's engagement with you. What might you say, specifically? What values are influencing your word choices and the sincerity of their delivery?

3. Next, your job is to *acknowledge* what the speaker said. What might you say to let them know you heard them sincerely and accurately? Does your response include your intention to validate, to report truthfully on the speaker's content and emotions, and to be open to being corrected if you got it wrong? Which values might be useful here?

4. You are now ready to uncover the *impact*. How might you refrain from becoming arrested by surface-level, reactive emotions? How might you resist the pull to reject, discredit, or invalidate the other person? In what ways could you hold on to your original goal as things get more messy and challenging? How might you dig even deeper, to access your vulnerable feelings and experiences? From this place, what would you say? What values might help you here?

5. Finally, what message of *hope* might you communicate to let the other person know you are committed to continuing this important work with them?

Avoiding Common Pitfalls

Now let's acknowledge some common pitfalls that can abound in this step and how you might manage them.

Hidden Expectations

The first common pitfall occurs when your hidden expectations take over. These expectations are usually different from your goals. While goals are designed to help you engage in constructive conversations, hidden expectations might unintentionally sabotage their success. Examples of hidden expectations include expecting an apology no matter what, expecting to win an argument, and expecting that all will go according to your plan.

Given your intention to be open to the perspectives and experiences of the other person, holding firmly to such expectations could easily get in the way of receiving fully.

You don't think so? This can't be you? Test yourself. Consider the following scenarios:

- You bring your special sweet potato pie to a family gathering and ask cousin Michael for his honest opinion about how it tastes.

- You suspect that there might be something going on with your teenage daughter, so you sit her down and ask her to be honest with you, and that she can and should tell you anything and everything.

- It's time for your annual review at work. Before your boss gets started, you insist you don't want her to sugar coat anything, that you are great with receiving honest and critical feedback.

Imagine yourself in each of these scenarios, and answer the following questions:

- What might be some hidden expectations you have in each of these cases? Maybe Michael's suggestion that you enter your pie in a contest because it's just that good? Maybe some expressed gratitude for being a great mom who cares? Or maybe your boss's minor constructive feedback about your occasional tardiness to work, but otherwise appreciation for being a dedicated employee?

- You are soliciting an honest response, but do you *really* want one? Would you be able to handle *anything* that the other person offers? Including maybe that your pie does not taste as good as you think it does? Maybe that your teenage daughter would like you to take her to get birth control? Or that maybe your tardiness is a serious concern for your boss?

- Could you imagine letting go of your expectations, to create room for whatever honest responses may come?

As suggested above, in the case of constructive conversations, unknowingly you may be forecasting a variety of responses and outcomes. These might include: "Now that I have informed them about their microaggression, they should apologize for what they did," "They should thank me for having the patience and taking the time to educate them—not everyone would," and "They should follow my lead and talk to me calmly and respectfully."

These kinds of shoulds and expectations can occur prior to, during, or even after the other person has responded. No matter when they manifest, they are not unreasonable. After all, you took a deliberate risk to initiate this difficult dialogue because the matter is of great importance to you. So of course you are invested in the outcome. It's perfectly understandable that you have expectations and hopes about how this will and should unfold. However, if permitted to take over, such presumptions can bring considerable trouble and seriously thwart your efforts to fully receive the other person's sharing.

UNCOVERING HIDDEN EXPECTATIONS

But you ask, "How can I see what is hidden?" Fair question. You're right, of course. If they are hidden expectations, how can you be expected to know about them? The answer is quite simple.

Most of us operate with some level of hidden expectations throughout various aspects of our lives. It might be the hidden wish of wanting others to find us desirable—as friends, lovers, or colleagues—but pretending and telling ourselves we don't care about others' opinions. Or wanting to win something—maybe a race, an argument, a prize—but convincing ourselves and those around us that what matters most is the effort and camaraderie. Or even the hidden craving that there could be some absolute guarantee about the future—such as our health, safety, and success—in spite of knowing that this is not possible, no matter how great our present effort.

It's not uncommon to tell ourselves slightly incomplete versions of our truths, like the ones above. We do so to protect ourselves from possible, and even probable, disappointment, hurt, and pain. Of course many of us are inclined to ignore, deny, or even suppress such hidden desires. But this only tightens their grip on us. Left hidden and unattended, they ultimately get in our way.

So how to excavate these hidden desires? We can uncover them quite readily by simple inquiries: *What am I really wishing for? What do I honestly want to happen? What do I secretly desire but am too afraid or embarrassed to admit?* Once uncovered, be sure to tend to these expectations, and yourself, with kindness. Hear them out. Reassure them. And then let them go.

You Can't Handle the Truth

Another pitfall involves the common experience of memory loss. At this phase of the journey, you can become vulnerable to forgetting that the ultimate goal of having a constructive conversation is to have the courage to speak and hear the truth: yours *and* theirs. Only through sharing truths and seeking understanding— instead of hiding behind our emotional fragility or politically (in) correct veneers—will we be able to take concerted and meaningful steps toward collective healing.

Recall that, leading up to this point, the following sequence transpired. With some forethought and planning, you invited someone to take a risk to engage in a difficult dialogue. You then shared your truth and leaned into the other person, relating your willingness to hear their truth. What this means now is that you actually have to be willing, not only to hear the other person's honest response, but also to genuinely acknowledge and believe it as *their* truth. Again, this does not mean you have to agree with them.

You might ask, "But what if what they are saying is really *not* true!?" It might certainly be the case that what you hear is in fact wrong information. For example, maybe the other person shares that sexism no longer exists in the US—maybe in other countries but definitely not in the US. Or they might say that people who are homeless don't deserve any government support, because they are all drug addicts. Or racial profiling is necessary to keep our communities safe. No doubt these statements are far from actual reality. They are, however, what the other person believes to be true.

If you shift your focus and efforts now to challenging and correcting their beliefs, you will find yourself on a sinking ship. In fact, we suspect this is familiar turf for many of you. This is often the point at which many of us get stuck: we get hijacked by our anger and outrage, and attempts at constructive conversations meet an untimely death.

Remember, at the core of constructive conversations is the hope and possibility of different people from different backgrounds, experiences, and identities coming together with mutual respect—not to criticize their differences but to connect, find common ground, and begin to heal in spite of these differences.

To this end, the goal of responding is to have the bravery to hear someone out, the courage to deepen your engagement, and the audacity to seek mutual understanding. This means respectfully giving space to the other person's thoughts, feelings, and experiences, without judgment or condemnation.

Instead of allowing an automatic response of outrage to get in the way, we encourage you to become curious. About how and why the other person has come to believe what they do. And about the deep impact of what they are saying has on you.

So, can you handle the truth? Your own, definitely. But what about the truth of the other person? Certainly, that's not as easy. It may even be painful. Yet having constructive conversations mandates that you resist the pull to reject, discredit, and invalidate the speaker's truth as they have shared it. Remember, we cannot heal as individuals, family, or community if we remain disconnected and afraid. If change and justice are what we are seeking, we must first do what others cannot or will not do: face one another, connect deeply and respectfully, and commit to working together. This is the necessary and critical precursor to changing any ideology, person, relationship, circumstance, and even our world.

Every constructive conversation leads us closer to these goals. Yes, it is a long-term endeavor. We will need to be endlessly patient and persistent. But it is worth the investment.

Back to Values

Each of the above common pitfalls may appear daunting at first blush. No doubt, letting go of our hidden expectations and accepting another's truth can feel like intimidating responsibilities. However, remember the powerful tool of values that you have at your disposal.

The value of *gratitude* can help in acknowledging, and even appreciating, the willingness of another person to come along with you on a challenging, unpredictable expedition. *I feel grateful they stayed. I feel grateful I have the strength to do this.*

Similarly, the value of *faith* can soothe your anxieties about letting go of your hidden expectations and trusting that the two of you can and will journey the road less traveled with mutual respect and integrity. *I have faith in myself. I have faith in this process. I have faith in the other person.*

Finally, the value of *justice* may guide you to invite yourself and the other person to step away from the shadows of social politeness and political correctness, and shed the cloak of fear, to invite and embrace your mutual truths, spoken so rarely on matters related to our cultural divisions and perceived differences. *I believe in justice, so taking this risk is worth it. With unwavering diligence and resolve, justice will prevail.*

You can see how these values of gratitude, faith, and justice can be applicable to any pitfall. So anchor yourself in the ones that you previously identified or add any of these three to your list. Allow the values again to drive your journey, now and moving ahead.

Your Turn

Turn to your journal. Let's take a few minutes to explore how these common pitfalls resonate with you.

Consider the constructive conversation you hope to have in the near future. Imagine that you have just navigated the first six steps and you are now getting ready to respond. Envision and write down as much detail as possible about this scenario.

1. Imagine yourself acknowledging and respecting the other person's willingness to engage with you in this process. In what ways would this be difficult? What if you had a strongly negative initial reaction to what they shared in response to your action? How would you feel?

2. Write down some of your anticipated expectations and presumptions. Hopes and wishes? In your ideal vision, what does the person say or do? If all goes well, how should this exchange unfold? Can you imagine relaxing your attachment to, or even letting go of, these expectations?

3. Now deliberate on a few likely responses from the speaker. Consider an unfavorable response. Could you accept, in that moment, that such a negative response is their truth? In spite of how you feel, could you resist the pull to reject, discredit, or invalidate their truth?

4. What values might help guide you throughout this process?

Summary

We have now concluded a full cycle of the constructive conversation voyage. In the next step, we highlight the need to repeat the cycle. But for now, congratulations! You have completed a full lap of this journey. You have traversed the complex but now manageable step of responding. Mastery here will undoubtedly ensure your ability to complete more laps in the future.

Throughout this process, you have remained close to and harnessed your most invaluable tools. Values such as gratitude, faith, justice, patience, compassion, honesty, love, forgiveness, hope, mercy, and, of course, courage have been your constant, infallible street soldiers. They have supported you in strengthening your skills, carrying you many steps closer to new pathways to healing.

DO IT AGAIN!

Congrats! You've gotten through Steps 1–7. It's time to do your victory lap. Rather than avoiding the uncomfortable topics, which is so easy to do, you are doing the opposite. You are learning and practicing ways to talk about tough topics like race, gender, sexuality, and class, with openness and honesty.

Do you feel proud of yourself? Hope so! It is quite an accomplishment to get this far. The journey, however, isn't quite over. That's right: in Step 8 you will "do it again!" A one-time effort is just that—one single, isolated incident. One time can be powerful, but realistically, to have true impact requires more than a single conversation.

What we're proposing is not a robotic "rinse and repeat." Instead, doing it again involves reflecting on what happened in the previous steps so you can be clear about the reasons for engaging again. Recall in Step 7 that in most situations, "to be continued" is what usually follows one full cycle of a constructive conversation. Based on how things were left in Step 7, you can now make an informed choice about how to continue the conversation, and the journey you started. You can decide what to talk about and who to talk with next. You also can better maneuver around the roadblocks, or barriers, that might lead you to make a U-turn.

Take Time to Reflect

Part of making Step 8 successful is reflecting on what happened in Steps 1 through 7. It's a good time to ponder on what you've done and how it went. Maybe Steps 1 through 3 went really well, but then once the words traveled out of your mouth to your loved one, it all went downhill. Another popular place for a hiccup is when it is time to wait and listen. You were totally fine, staying in stride with the steps, until the person you were talking to came at you with the most ridiculous response you've ever heard. The last thing you wanted to do next was wait and listen, and so before you knew it, you went rogue. Or maybe the opposite is true. Maybe you had a constructive conversation that unfolded pretty much as you had planned and hoped. You feel very satisfied with the dialogue that transpired, but then out of nowhere new topics about culture and diversity emerged.

As these examples demonstrate, constructive conversations might need repeating for a myriad of reasons, including because they did not come to fruition during the first attempt or because they inspired new ideas or topics you want to pursue.

Here are some ways to reflect:

1. Use the mindfulness and grounding skills you learned earlier in this book to settle your mind, and bring awareness to how you felt during and, now, after the constructive conversation. Now that you've given the first constructive conversation a try, how does your body feel? Scan from head to toe, and notice any new or different feelings. Pay attention to how your body feels now compared to how it felt during the conversation. If you feel unsettled, nervous, or angry, or if you have any other looming feelings, take some deep breaths to ground yourself in the present moment. Go back to your values and take refuge in them. No matter what the outcome of the constructive conversation, you started from a place of genuine and virtuous intentions. If you feel relieved, content, or even relaxed, enjoy it! There is no right or wrong in how you feel at the end of the constructive conversation. Instead, it's all part of the process, so take it all in.

And trust that it will help you to decide how to eventually move forward.

2. Schedule a time to reflect. Close your eyes and mentally review the constructive conversation you just had. Think about the parts you feel satisfied with and parts that need more work. For the successful parts—awesome! Where you had missteps, commit to more practicing. For those of you who are verbal processers, you might consider debriefing with someone you trust. Sharing out loud what you experienced can make a big difference in deepening your insight.

Rather than having the constructive conversation be a "one and done" event, thoughtful reflection on Steps 1 through 7 can bring important insight and propel you into more constructive conversations in the future. Mistakes or omissions in the steps can guide you to where you might want to go next. We strongly encourage you to engage in a thorough analysis before deciding what, when, and how Step 8 will take place. Don't hesitate to sleep on it. Time can be your friend in eventually seeing things from a new perspective, including possible "aha" moments from the initial constructive conversation.

Just after having a constructive conversation, and before doing it again, we recommend the following:

Do:

- Take time for self-care—go on a walk or hike, take a bath, read a book, meet a friend, or simply rest. Engaging in constructive conversations can be depleting, so it's important that you recharge your energy.

- Schedule time to marinate and ponder on the constructive conversation experience you just had.

- Use your journal to jot down important reflections and takeaways.

Don't:

- Overthink or overanalyze what just happened. (Not easy, but a good skill to aspire to.)

- Judge yourself critically if the constructive conversation didn't go as you planned or hoped. (Remember the gifts of imperfection!)

- Blame or demonize the other person if the constructive conversation didn't go well. (Others are imperfect too!)

- Avoid or vow to never engage in another constructive conversation. (Wanting distance from a challenging or "failed" experience is understandable, but don't forget, any goal worth aspiring to requires time, patience, and diligence, "Success" for the Kim Constructive Conversations Model is not about having a flawless dialogue. Rather, it is about your commitment to the journey for the long haul.)

Reworking Missteps

A common reason for the necessity of Step 8 is that we rarely, if ever, implement all of the steps as flawlessly or precisely as we had envisioned. By taking an honest look at how things went, you can then decide what to do again and what to modify in the future. The following prompts will help you reflect on the effectiveness of the constructive conversation you just had.

Missed the Goal

If you don't think your initial goal was met, you might consider making a second attempt. Like a research hypothesis, a poorly worded goal can lead to faulty results. Therefore, an unmet goal may mean that your goal needs to be reworded or reframed.

Let's consider again the case of Anna. If Anna's conversation with her parents went south, it would be fruitful to reexamine how she set up her initial goal. For example, if Anna's goal was to convince her parents that Mohammed really is a good fit for her, then she would have likely felt defeated, frustrated, and even angry if her parents did not change their minds.

Similarly, if Anna's goal was to get her parents to feel happy for her, she would have likely felt discontent when her parents expressed their disapproval. You probably noticed that both of these goals are very other-focused.

So when revisiting, Anna might set a goal that focuses more on her own words and actions. A revised goal for Anna might be *I want to let my parents know that I am not worried about the religious and cultural differences between me and Mohammed, and actually it is because of these differences that I learn so much from him.*

Your Turn

Now think about the constructive conversation you just completed but that didn't pan out so well. If the misstep was a goal that needs reworking, go back to your personal journal and rewrite the goal. When revising, consider the following:

- *What about your original goal do you think was ineffective?*

- *How can you rework your goal so that it is clear, specific, and realistic?*

- *Focus on outcomes that depend on you more than others.*

- *Consult with your buddy or another person you trust. Get their input about how you might reframe your goal to better reflect your intentions.*

- *Schedule a time when you will try out your new revised goal.*

Roadblocks Ahead

Even with solid preparation, there are just some barriers you might not be able to predict. You thought you anticipated every barrier imaginable, but then there was that one that came out of nowhere! You can't always know enough about the person you are speaking with to know what interpersonal barriers might arise between the two of you. With a stranger or acquaintance, this is especially true. You likely will not know what will be challenging about talking and listening to a store clerk, a neighbor, or the person on the subway until you are actually taking action. And if you are not the one starting the conversation, or you start a conversation on the spur of the moment, then you may not even have time to iden-tify barriers ahead of time.

If you find yourself in this scenario:

Do:

- Be kind to yourself. You are not a mind reader.

- Try to learn from the barrier, especially if you think it will come up again.

- Take deep breaths and ground when you are facing unex-pected challenges.

- Think outside the box when trying to anticipate roadblocks.

Don't:

- Beat yourself up about not catching this the first time.

- Get discouraged.

- Let the barriers win. Get back into the conversation when you are ready.

Empty Values

Values are the fuel in your gas tank. If you give your engine the wrong gasoline, or not enough gas, your car will not go far. If you found that your values did not keep you going over the long haul, go back to the drawing board. Try these tactics for brainstorming new values that will sustain you through these tough conversations:

- Ask yourself what keeps you going in the darkest of times. Use this to fill your tank.

- Look to your heroes and heroines...use their values as inspiration when you are running low.

- Select inspiring quotes or personal mantras to fill your tank.

- If you believe in a higher power, pray for clarity around what values will get you through this work.

Remember, this is bigger than just you, so let your higher principles keep you afloat.

Taking a Wrong Turn

Steps 4 through 7 are all about talking and listening. As you can imagine, plenty of wrong turns can occur during this phase. One quick daydream, and the person you are talking to could have missed your opener. Distractions and interruptions are common clogs in the communication wheel, and they can really take things down the wrong path.

When taking action, your actual words might not have completely matched the initial goal. Let's return to Anna's rendezvous with her parents. After listening to her parents' response, Anna may not be able to effectively acknowledge their reaction. Anna's will is there, but the words won't come out. When these snafus happen, the key is not to beat yourself up. Show yourself compassion and then eventually get back in the game.

Anna may decide that the next time she broaches a constructive conversation with her parents, she actually wants to invite Mohammed to be there too. By having Mohammed be part of the conversation, she is taking action in a new way. Family therapists might say this action is changing the equilibrium in the family. The family system has no choice but to recalibrate, and with it comes new opportunities for new dialogue.

Alicia's Turn

Not too long ago, I proudly posted a photograph of my mom, my dad, and me on social media on Loving Day, celebrating the Supreme Court decision that it was officially illegal to ban interracial marriages in the United States. My parents were an interracial couple in the 1970s, and sharing the photo was a way that I connected and felt a part of this important landmark. My mom, on the other hand, did not like that I posted this photo publicly since my parents are divorced and she has long since remarried. For me, I felt like my mom was saying she wanted to erase a part of our past, which is a sentiment that I found deeply hurtful. It was a tough conversation, and we just did not see eye to eye.

At times, we went down a rabbit hole, and we went in circles too. So, what is the lesson of this story? Don't be friends with your mom on Facebook!

All joking aside, it was a genuine exchange, and there were some positive results from the conversation, even though it did deviate from the steps. For example, the following Mother's Day, my mom gave me a card with a woman of color on the front. It may seem like a small gesture, but I read this as my mother's way of saying she sees me. My mom was deliberately trying to recognize and celebrate my brownness, which comes from being a multiracial person.

Let this reassure you that each step does not have to be adhered to flawlessly for some positive outcome. Considering our first conversation was over the phone, I'd also like to "do it again" in person, perhaps sitting down over a mother-daughter lunch to talk. That is, I want to initiate another constructive conversation with my mom about the meaning of the photo to me and to better understand her perspective as well. To be continued!

Your Turn

Think about someone in your life who is worth you doing it again with. You may find yourself wanting to try again with someone because of the value you place on the relationship. As you can imagine, family and friends often fall under this umbrella. Having constructive conversations with those we care about is a process. Building personal and interpersonal skills that allow us to do this is not easy—it takes time and also practice.

1. In your journal, write down their names. List the reasons why you want to try again with each person you named.

2. Next, go to these people and tell them they are important to you. Share with them how you feel. Let them know that you want to talk with them openly about things that are important to you, on an ongoing basis. By doing this, you are increasing the chances of having successful future constructive conversations with them.

We strongly encourage you to identify which skills you found especially challenging, and work on practicing those skills. Don't let the fact that the first constructive conversation didn't go flawlessly prevent you from trying again. Instead, use it at as a catalyst for future conversations.

Repeating with the Same and Different People

Build a house, then a village, and then a world of constructive conversations. While you start with one constructive conversation, the process of the first one will guide you to another and then another. This ongoing approach has a tendency to really build up those conversational muscles. It also increases the possibility for real change and healing.

Let's get a little more specific. You can repeat constructive conversations in two primary ways: First, you can revisit or continue a constructive conversation with the same person at another point in time. Second, you can pursue a constructive conversation with a different person. Of course these conversations with the same or different person could be on the same, related, or different topics.

Following Up with the Same Person

Remember Tim and Rose in their workplace. Tim initiated a constructive conversation with Rose about diversity, equity, and inclusion because of the differing perspectives they had about hiring the Black applicant. When "doing it again," Tim can decide to continue this conversation in a variety of ways. First, he may decide to revisit the conversation with Rose by scheduling a time to follow up with her directly. In this follow-up, Tim can share what insights and reflections he has had since their initial conversation as well as invite Rose to share any additional perspectives she may have.

Here are some ways Tim might broach the issue again with Rose:

- "Rose, I really appreciated the talk we had. I've been thinking a lot about what you said and what we discussed. It wasn't easy, but I think we started to make some movement. If you're up for it, I would love to continue our talk. I really appreciated hearing where you were coming from and would like to see where we can go moving forward. When are you free to grab some coffee?"

- "Rose, I realize things got a bit awkward between you and me after our talk. I know you were not happy that the company ended up hiring the Black applicant. The conversation that you and I had was definitely hard, but I still think it was very important and necessary. In fact, I wish we could all be more open and honest at work as you and I were. I'm curious if you have had any reflections since then. I certainly have. If you're open to it, I would love to hear how you have been feeling since our talk."

Tim could also keep it simple:

- "Rose, what ideas have come up for you since our last conversation about increasing diversity at the our company? I would love to hear them."

- "Rose, how have you been since our last conversation? I know strong emotions came up for both of us, and so I wanted to touch base and check in. I really appreciated your openness and willingness to hear me out."

The time span between the first and consecutive constructive conversations can really vary. Tim may want to check in the next day, week, month, or even longer. It's ok to give yourself the time needed to engage again. The key is knowing that in most circumstances, meaningful and lasting impact requires continuous effort.

Another possible option is for Tim to ask Rose if she would be open to dedicating a time once per month, or perhaps once per quarter, to discuss broader issues pertaining to diversity, equity, and inclusion. They can dedicate time to engage in constructive conversations about hiring and other objectives for the company, as well as their own working relationship. This format for an ongoing, dedicated time for constructive conversations could be a way Tim and Rose can also address new topics pertaining to culture and diversity that are important to both of them.

Following Up with a Different Person

Tim can participate in Step 8 in a way that doesn't directly involve Rose. He can continue the constructive conversation by tackling the same issue but with a different person or even a group of people. Having become very invested in the importance of workplace diversity, Tim might decide to have more constructive conversations with whoever is willing to engage. His comfort level and confidence in effectively navigating such conversations have grown as a result of his challenging but successful conversation with Rose.

Tim might decide to raise this issue explicitly with members of future hiring committees. He might also initiate constructive conversations with other coworkers—maybe in one-on-one meetings in order to exchange ideas about how the company can improve their diversity, equity, and inclusion efforts. Furthermore, motivated to make additional positive systemic change, Tim might also decide to pursue this dialogue with administrative staff, including his own boss. Finally, he might even bring his newfound skills home, where he could broach constructive conversations with family members on culture and diversity matters they have long disagreed on.

Hopefully, knowing you can do the steps again, with the same or different person, will encourage and empower you to do just that.

Doing More and Better

After completing one full cycle of a constructive conversation, you might be feeling very motivated to continue this journey. Maybe you even catch the constructive conversation bug! If this is the case, we strongly encourage you to start developing a plan. The nature of these difficult dialogues makes it so that unless there is deliberate intention, it will become easy to slip back into old habits and status quo. So, if you are really serious about all of this and you're ready to go deeper, here are some reasons and ways to make a plan!

Why Plan?

"Why do I need a plan?" you ask. You need a plan because having constructive conversations is not easy. It's hard work! Having *effective* constructive conversations is a skill—and developing any new skill is also not easy. It requires time, patience, and practice. So, if you *really* want to do this well and be able to repeat it many times, you need a game plan.

You might still be asking, "Why not just do it when a situation arises?" Because you want to make this easier on yourself, not harder! One of the reasons these conversations are so difficult is that we don't engage in them nearly enough. Add to that the sensitive nature of the topics involved (e.g., racism, heterosexism), and it's no wonder we choose to delay or even avoid these conversations altogether. That is, until the problems again become too big to ignore.

Having a plan will allow you to build your new skills, have opportunities to practice them, and ultimately be better prepared and more effective when the time comes to utilize them, even under urgent circumstances.

How Do I Plan?

First, identify your purpose. This purpose should be broad. Maybe ask yourself again why you picked up this book. What bigger aspiration are you seeking?

Next, identify who, what, when, where, why, and how you will continue to build your constructive conversation skills. The more detailed and explicit the plan, the greater the likelihood it will translate from aspiration to reality. As suggested above, the plan could lead to more in-depth engagement with the same or different person, topic, or context. There is abundant room to do it your way, with whomever you want, on a topic of your choosing, and when and where you want to engage.

Maybe your goal is to zero in on your family. You can plan to have constructive conversations with various family members— whenever, wherever, and with whomever. Your plan would involve having constructive conversations big and small, at every family gathering, on any topic of social injustice, and with any and every family member willing to engage. When you have the courage to have such conversations with those you love the most, and with whom you have the most to lose, you reap the most direct benefits if you can be brave and diligent in your commitment.

Finally, write down your plan in your journal. Then share it with someone you trust so you can receive support and also keep yourself accountable. The idea here is to take small but intentional steps in the direction of your plan. You don't want to get lost or derailed by any one situation. You're in it for the long haul and for big change, which is not easy but most definitely worthwhile. Maybe you can encourage your accountability buddy to also develop their own personal plan. Success can be enhanced when you're doing it together.

Practice Makes Perfect

Your mother was right—practice does make perfect. Okay, maybe not perfect, but definitely better. At the heart of your individualized plan's success is practice, practice, practice.

So how to practice? There is no right or wrong way. However, consistency and diligence matter. With that in mind, here are some suggestions:

1. Commit to doing it regularly.

2. Don't wait until there is an imminent crisis.

3. Make it a *have-to*.

4. Practice every day. That's right, *every* day. It doesn't need to be a big ordeal or take up a ton of your time. It can become routine, like brushing your teeth. Do it at work, at school, with a stranger on the bus, during carpool, waiting in line to check out your groceries, at the gas station, with a coworker in a staff meeting, during coffee break, at the dinner table or with the bank teller. You may not even have the full constructive conversation, but you can practice any one or more of the steps and accompanying tools in the model, including of course deep listening.

5. Expect mistakes—we all make them! They make you more humble and relatable.

6. Be kind to yourself; be your own best cheerleader.

7. Engage in ongoing self-reflection—what went well, what needs more work?

8. And as we've said before, include others in the process. There is strength in numbers.

Challenges and Benefits

While we are encouraging you to have these conversations again and again, we also realize that there are real barriers to acknowledge. These barriers can be very practical constraints, like lack of time and fatigue. We live in an era of busy lives, and slowing down to engage in constructive conversations can feel antithetical to your lifestyle. Wouldn't it just be easier for you to keep going about your day rather than to pause and address these things?

Having these sorts of conversations, especially in the beginning, takes some forethought, and forethought takes time. These conversations can also easily trigger old and even recent wounds and evoke strong feelings deep within us, all of which can be overwhelming and even exhausting. Many of us are conditioned to avoid pain, and so naturally may dodge conversations that might remind us of our unresolved traumas. Therefore, there may be times you intentionally decide to not engage in a constructive conversation, even when the opportunity clearly presents itself. You simply might be too hurt, raw, or depleted...and those are all valid reasons to not engage.

With practice however, it can and will get easier—even as we battle through our own unsettled wounds and pain. In fact, as we indicated throughout this book, ongoing constructive conversations can lead to personal healing and transformation. Applying the steps again and again can facilitate clarity and invite a profound sense of empowerment and liberation. You may find yourself getting lighter with each conversation, because you are holding less back. There is relief in knowing you are actively working on and addressing things important to you in your life. You are walking the walk and talking the talk. Ongoing constructive conversations can also attenuate difficult emotions, such as anger and resentment, because you are broaching things more directly, honestly, and courageously. You can rest easier because you are living a life in which your actions are aligned with your values.

Lastly, you may find that others are noticing and complimenting you on your new skills! We have heard comments such as "Just wanted to send you some props for handling that situation perfectly!"

and "You were clear while also being compassionate." Getting nice feedback is not why you do it, but it is rewarding to know that you're making a positive impact on others.

Truly, the more you do it, the more benefits you will experience in your own life and in the lives of those around you.

Summary

You can change the world one constructive conversation at a time, but one conversation alone won't do it. Hopefully, the reality that the steps are designed to be repeated doesn't feel overwhelming. Remember, you can take breaks and set your own pace. But we must keep marching on.

Writing down and carrying out your individualized plan will help you feel prepared for continuing what you started with this book. With purpose, you can navigate your way through all kinds of situations, even when you don't know beforehand exactly what they will look like or how they will unfold.

And by your example you will inspire others to do the same. Only together can we build our community, through the courage to speak, listen, and act.

CONSTRUCTIVE CONVERSATIONS AS A LIFESTYLE

Wow, you did it! You made it through all 8 steps of the Kim Constructive Conversations Model. Pat yourself on your back. Seriously. You deserve it.

But don't get too comfortable. The work is still not over. In fact, you have only just embarked on this journey. What lies ahead will certainly test your stamina and resolve more times than you'll care to count. But the potential for healing yourself and your relationships, as well as the world around you, will be boundless. So set your aspirations high, and make sure your reach exceeds your grasp.

In this conclusion, you will realize that in addition to talking, civic engagement is required. This may take the form of volunteering, citizenship, service, or advocacy. We will also explore ways to make constructive conversations even more impactful and rewarding in the long run by making them part of your lifestyle.

Talking Is Not Enough

Yes, we know, this book that you are just about done reading has been all about talking and listening. So why, at the very end, are we suggesting that that's not enough? Well, because it's not. Talking and listening *alone* are not enough—not when the problems we're up against are racism, classism, sexism, ableism, heterosexism, and xenophobia. These are institutional oppressions embedded into the fabric of our social, political, and cultural systems, which disproportionately and unfairly advantage some at the expense of others.

We're not just talking about a preference for one group of people over another. It's a matter of fundamental human rights, safety, and dignity. People are being traumatized and even losing their lives over these issues.

So, no, talking and listening alone are not enough. They are a critical beginning and launching pad. But if systemic change and justice are what you are seeking, you must amplify your efforts, by including intentional civic engagement alongside constructive conversations.

We understand that all of this might feel overwhelming. But don't worry. We're not expecting you to run for political office tomorrow (although, hey, why not?). We do, however, expect that you will consider your own role and responsibility in how oppression becomes propagated and reinforced. Quite frankly, we all have a part in this. And we can and must do something about it.

Get Involved

You might not consider yourself someone who gets involved. Maybe you like to lay low and only offer your time when you absolutely *have* to. We admit, getting involved can be messy, hard, and time-consuming. But we hope you'll agree it's also necessary.

The fact that you picked up this book suggests that you are someone who can do it. In fact, we all have much more potential than we realize. Ordinary people do extraordinary things every day.

A few months ago, there was a news article about a Black grocery employee who allowed a white teen with autism to help him shelve cartons of orange juice. Noticing how mesmerized the teen was, the employee asked him if he'd like to help. The teen was ecstatic and began to shelve the juice cartons under the gentle direction of the employee. In a culture where people with disabilities are often ignored or dismissed, and against the national backdrop of persistent racial tensions, this small and intimate gesture proved transformative for the teen. The grocery employee, a young man in his early twenties, was himself also unexpectedly moved to tears by his ability to validate and make another person so happy.

Stories like this, especially when they involve young people who have nothing tangible to gain, give us hope. They also remind us that in our own way we can and must do our part to change the world.

WHAT WOULD YOU DO?

What would you do if presented with a situation to get involved? If you haven't already, check out the ABC television show *What Would You Do?* hosted by John Quiñones. Using hidden cameras, unsuspecting people are confronted with everyday dilemmas, including those that involve mistreatment of culturally disenfranchised persons. What would *you* do if you observed a group of teens taunting a homeless person? If the restaurant in which you are dining refused service to a family with gay parents? Or if a sales clerk followed and questioned a Black patron for no apparent reason?

For those who didn't get involved, many reported wanting to do so but didn't due to discomfort or fear of potential consequences. We suspect many of you can relate. However, those who did stand up and got involved in these scenarios later reported feeling angry, nervous, and uncertain, even as they found themselves engaging. In fact, many were visibly shaken. But in the end, their deep sense of moral conscience and courage prevailed.

Watching others in action can be very motivating. The brave gestures of others, no matter how small, can be contagious. So be on the lookout for others in action in your everyday life. Be inspired. You can do it too!

Beyond the day-to-day situations that may or may not happen to you, we implore you to get involved, deliberately and proactively. Don't wait for the have-to scenario. An honest look at the world around you should affirm that now is the time to speak up, stand up, and get involved. Find something you feel passionate about. Maybe gender equity, health care, education, gun violence, child abuse, climate change, unemployment, poverty or civil rights. What could you do, in your own way, to take action? In your family? Your school or work? Your place of worship? Your neighborhood or community? Go ahead—dream big *and* small. Imagine you can. Imagine you will.

Small actions, as well as those by a single individual, can lead to big changes. Remember Harvey Milk, Rosa Parks, Malala Yousafzai, Alicia Garza, or the young activists from Marjory Stoneman Douglas High School, who used tragedy to birth a social movement. These folks stepped up in extraordinary ways, but don't forget: they were just as ordinary as any one of us. They simply and boldly believed in their convictions to do the right thing. Without a doubt, they must have been scared and even uncertain at times, but, again, remember that courage is what we do in the face of fear. We are each capable of this. Turn to the many role models around you to find inspiration.

Here are some suggestions for getting involved. If your time is limited, you can:

- Contribute financially to organizations that champion specific social causes.

- Participate in a protest, walk out, or rally.

- Help with voter registration—remember, we can and do have a voice.

- Volunteer in your local community (e.g., schools, food banks, homeless shelters, or girls and boys clubs).

- Write letters to or hold town hall meetings with your legislators.

- Boycott businesses and organizations that mistreat or exploit workers, or employ unjust policies and practices (e.g., unfair wages or culture of sexual harassment).

If you have the luxury of time—well, the sky's the limit. In addition to contributing to organizations of your choosing, you might also:

- Get involved in organizing local and national social justice movements.

- Serve on the hiring committee at your school or workplace to recruit diverse and historically underrepresented people.

- Develop and provide low-cost or pro bono training and education on important social issues (e.g., ableism, racism, heterosexism, sexism, or xenophobia).

- Volunteer to serve on your child's PTA and help create an inclusive community for all families.

- Invest your time and money in disenfranchised neighborhoods and communities (e.g., support local businesses, hire local workers, or live in diverse neighborhoods).

- Offer low-cost or pro bono services in your areas of expertise to marginalized communities (e.g., legal, medical, art, therapy, education, or sports).

- Recruit coworkers, friends, and family to do any or all of the above with you. Build a community of activists! Healing work is infectious.

As you can see, there is no limit to how you can get involved. But instead of becoming overwhelmed by the enormity of possibilities, we advise that you start small, close to home. In fact, involvement with your family, neighborhood, and community can be more powerful than writing a check from a distance. When you commit sincerely and engage deeply with those around you, you will also reap the bountiful benefits of your efforts. As Mother Teresa once said, "Love begins at home." So start with those closest to you: your family, friends, and neighbors.

When you get involved, you encounter more opportunities to have constructive conversations. In turn, your talking and listening skills will inevitably strengthen. You will become more comfortable and will experience more success in connecting honestly with others. It will become your new normal.

Make Engagement a Way of Life

Why do we suggest that you make this a way of life? Because institutional oppression is insidious, deceptive, and omnipotent. It is like an endless valley of weeds, designed to breed more weeds. So, if you are serious about healing yourself and those around you, constructive conversations and civic engagement must become a way of life. Singular or even occasional attempts will be inadequate in yielding lasting change. At best, they will only be temporary, a fleeting respite. Around the corner will be more weeds, waiting to take over.

Every one of us can become complicit in institutionalized systems of oppression. We live in a world in which injustice and disparities abound. This breeds fertile grounds for misunderstanding, disconnection, anger, pain, and othering. If we don't actively resist the proliferation of weeds, they will continue to grow bigger and stronger. They will creep back into our mind-set and reinforce the oppression. Thus, you have to make concerted changes in your lifestyle for any seeds of justice you plant to have a fighting chance.

But How?

At first blush, the thought of constructive conversations and civic engagement as a way of life might feel intimidating. It's not. It's purely about mind-set and repetition.

Hear us out. When you practice constructive conversations regularly, they *will* become a way of life. When you work faithfully with others to stand up for injustice, that *will* become a way of life. It really is as simple as taking one step at a time. As the Chinese philosopher Lao Tzu noted, "A journey of a thousand miles begins with a single step." One foot in front of the other. One conversation, one civic engagement after another. Again and again.

Imagine starting a new exercise program. At first, you commit to exercising just one day. In spite of how fantastic that workout might have felt, you know your overall health will not benefit if you stop there. So, you gradually expand to multiple days or even daily exercising—something sustainable, maybe a twenty-minute morning walk around your neighborhood. You start to notice and connect with other morning walkers. Knowing you are not alone motivates you to stay on your program.

Before you know it, and maybe even without intending to, you become a morning walker—it becomes your new way of life. In fact, you find yourself now making healthier choices at mealtimes. You even try out meditation, to further ease your daily stress. Over time, your health improves markedly, as does your capacity to engage in vigorous exercise if and when you choose.

A HAVE-TO MIND-SET

Indeed, the leap to a have-to mind-set and a way of life is actually no leap at all. Rather, it is an intentional and methodical step, preceded by many steps and followed by successive steps.

Still think it's too much? Let's pause briefly and consider the endless have-to's that you have chosen to make part of your life. This includes everything from brushing your teeth and taking a shower to making dinner, doing laundry, and going to school or work. Most likely it also includes filing your taxes every year and standing in line at the DMV.

We bet most if not all of you do these things. Regardless of whether you like or want to do any or all of these activities, the reality is that you choose to do them. You probably feel like you have to do them. But honestly, you don't have to brush your teeth or shower. Sure, you might get more cavities, and your body odor and lack of hygiene might lead to social rejection. But it's not against the law to not do it. And even if it were, you still don't have to do it.

These are all choices you make, some more difficult than others. But it was your choice to make it your have-to. In so doing, it has simply become your way of life—something you don't need to debate or deliberate about every time. You know it's important, so you do it. Period.

If you think about it, racism, classism, heterosexism, ableism, sexism, and xenophobia all involve more dire and grave consequences than not brushing your teeth or taking a shower, or even not filing your taxes or renewing your driver's license. Sure, you might have to pay fines, or even serve some jail time for tax evasion or driving with an expired license. Definitely not small consequences. However, with the oppressions we listed, you could be injured, assaulted, or even die as a result.

It stands to reason that matters that involve anyone's fundamental dignity and safety must be a have-to—for all of our sake. Choosing not to get involved cannot be an option.

Consider this final analogy. Any form of oppression is essentially in opposition to everything we attempt to teach our kids: be kind, keep your hands to yourself, share, say sorry, work hard, play fair, be an ally, and don't give up. Oppressing others who look, love, believe, move, and do things differently is not kind, respectful, helpful, or fair. In fact, to teach our children one thing and behave ourselves in another way is at a minimum very confusing and, frankly, not good parenting.

We are not suggesting that you are actively behaving unkindly, unfairly, or disrespectfully. Or for those to whom it applies, that you are a bad parent. Rather, we are hoping to illuminate the deceptive ways in which oppression works—to get "good" people to enact its deeds, through ignorance and inactivity. Without lifting a finger, we are colluding through our silence and inaction. As Dr. Martin Luther King Jr. wrote, "History will have to record that the greatest tragedy of this period of social transition was not the strident clamor of the bad people, but the appalling silence of the good people." We have to unmute ourselves. We can't lay low. We have to get involved.

If you are hearing this for the first time, please don't be too hard on yourself. You are not alone. We all have a part in this. Just as raising a child is a formidable responsibility, so too is healing long-standing, painful wounds. But just as a parent doesn't abandon their child through the inevitable ups and downs of parenting (including adolescence!), we too must stick it out. Remember, it's an investment.

We hope our children live up to the aspirations we teach them. So that they have a fighting chance, we have to do our part in ensuring that they inherit a world in which these aspirations are possible. To this end, we must become good role models. Frankly, we haven't always been the best role models. We can do more. We have to do more. We have to do better. You don't have to be a child psychologist to know that "Do as I say and not as I do" is *not* a good parenting method.

We must lead by example. We must be kind, keep our hands to ourselves, share, say sorry, work hard, play fair, be an ally, and don't give up. Our efforts will be worth it.

Grow Your Garden

We hope it's clear by now that constructive conversations are not a one-shot deal. They are not a quick fix. Healing, even from a paper cut, takes time. So be patient. A single constructive conversation becoming a way of life requires time.

Think of it as a beautiful garden that you intend to grow. You will plant seeds (constructive conversations and civic engagement) to be watered every day. Some days you might need to be more attentive, as strong winds and belligerent weeds threaten the survival of your fledgling seeds. Other days, the sun will be abundant and will nourish their development with ease. But every day, no matter the conditions, you will care for them with unwavering devotion. With each watering, you will watch your seeds slowly but assuredly grow and ultimately blossom.

It will not happen overnight. But eventually, your faith and diligence will nurture them into bloom. Before long your family and friends will notice your dedication and the fruits of your labor. Inspired, they will join you, and start a garden of their own. With time, a community of gardeners will develop, and with them the possibility of a beautiful world.

Final Thoughts

We hope that by reading this book you have become more confident in your ability to have constructive conversations about culture and diversity. The eight steps we discussed in this book are not a panacea. However, they can and will provide much-needed comfort, direction, and grounding to help you get started and to support you when you need it most. They will also provide the structure to help you grow, even in the absence of imminent crisis. In this way, your skills and success will flourish.

Remember, the Kim Constructive Conversations Model should not be utilized as a rigid manual. Rather, allow it to guide your process. Along the way, you might discover your own unique adaptations, which reflect your personal needs and style. There is lots of room to make this process your own.

Even though we touched on a number of oppressions, there are others that also deserve attention. The beauty of this model is that it can be generalized to other isms and difficult topics. So don't be shy. Try this in any area of your life.

Finally, hold on to your values, the heart of this model! They are the water that will nurture your garden.

Happy planting!

Acknowledgments

Thank you to our husbands, children, parents, sisters, and the many other family members who have been there for us through thick and thin. Thank you to the generations before us, who sacrificed so that we could have the opportunities we have now to write, teach, counsel, and heal.

Thank you to Anatasia's mother, Ahn Ok Sun, who bequeathed the audacious spirit and power of the Jeju women, and to her father, Kim Young Cho, who teaches every day that courage can be kind, patient, and forgiving.

Thank you to Alicia's mother, Judy Sarao, who believed in her from the beginning, and to her father, Norman del Prado, who instilled in her the value of lifelong learning. And thank you to Joel Boquiren for understanding that writing needed to happen even when we were in the Bahamas.

Thank you to Ryan Buresh, Caleb Beckwith, and all of the editors at New Harbinger. We will forever appreciate your patience and passion during this process, and for seeing the potential in the Kim Constructive Conversations Model. You guided us through transforming our academic writing styles into understandable prose. We are so grateful.

Thank you to Dr. Kevin Nadal and Shebani Patel Baniheshemi for reviewing this book in its early stages. We took to heart your grounding, insightful, and honest feedback, and this book is truly better because of your candor.

Thank you to New Harbinger for welcoming our book to your notable collection of amazing publications. For years, we have assigned your books in our classes and recommended them to our clients. It is an honor to join your team of authors.

Thank you to the Wright Institute, our academic home, and to the students, faculty, staff, and administration, who inspire and challenge us daily to be the best psychologists we can be.

REFERENCES

Eckel, S. 2017. "Divider-in-Chief: Love Him or Hate Him, People Are Striving to Manage the Trump-Related Rifts in Their Relationships." *Psychology Today.* https://www.psychologytoday.com/us/articles/201705/divider-in-chief.

Graham, S. 2006. *Diversity: Leaders Not Labels.* New York, New York: Simon and Schuster.

King, Martin Luther, Jr. "Address at the Fourth Annual Institute on Nonviolence and Social Change." Speech, Birmingham, AL, December 3, 1959. https://kinginstitute.stanford.edu/king-papers/documents/address-fourth-annual-institute-nonviolence-and-social-change-bethel-baptist-0.

Lickona, T. 2004. *Character Matters: How to Help Our Children Develop Good Judgment, Integrity, and Other Essential Virtues.* New York: Simon and Schuster.

Luft, J. M., and H. Ingham. 1955. *The Johari Window: A Graphic Model of Interpersonal Awareness.* Proceedings of the Western Training Laboratory in Group Development. Los Angeles: University of California, Los Angeles.

Norcross, J. C., and M. J. Lambert. 2018. "Psychotherapy Relationships That Work III." *Psychotherapy,* 55(4): 303–315.

Oliphant, B., and S. Smith. 2016. "How Americans Are Talking About Trump's Election in 6 Charts." Pew Research Center. http://www.pewresearch.org/fact-tank/2016/12/22/how-americans-are-talking-about-trumps-election-in-6-charts.

Singleton, G. E. 2015. *Courageous Conversations About Race: A Field Guide for Achieving Equity in Schools.* 2nd ed. Thousand Oaks, CA: Corwin Press.

Anatasia S. Kim, PhD, is a tenured associate professor at The Wright Institute in Berkeley, CA, where she also has a private practice specializing in treating adolescents and young adults. She is a National Ronald McNair Scholar and the recipient of numerous awards, including the American Psychological Association Minority Fellowship, Okura Mental Health Fellowship, and APAGS Guardian of Psychology Award. Kim has served as president of the Alameda County Psychological Association, chair of the California Psychological Association (CPA) Immigration Task Force, and diversity delegate of the CPA. She has presented and published in the areas of cultural competence and training, immigration, women of color in academia, and more.

Alicia del Prado, PhD, is a tenured associate professor at The Wright Institute in Berkeley, CA, and a licensed counseling psychologist with a private practice in Danville, CA. She has published numerous journal articles and chapters on cross-cultural psychology; personality; acculturation; and ethnic identity, including the first enculturation scale for Filipino Americans; and provides consultation and trainings on multicultural issues to companies and colleges. del Prado is chair and cofounder of the Asian American Psychology Association's (AAPA) Division on Asian Americans with Multiple Heritages, and was awarded both the Alameda County Psychological Association's Janet Hurwich Award and the AAPA Okura Community Leadership Award.

Foreword writer **Kevin L. Nadal, PhD**, is professor of psychology at both John Jay College of Criminal Justice, and the Graduate Center at the City University of New York. He received his doctorate in counseling psychology from Columbia University in New York City, NY. Nadal's research focuses on the impacts of microaggressions on the mental and physical health of people of color; lesbian, gay, bisexual, transgender, and queer (LGBTQ) people; and other marginalized groups.

MORE BOOKS *from*
NEW HARBINGER PUBLICATIONS

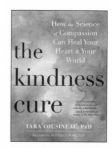

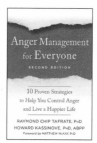

Register your **new harbinger** titles for additional benefits!

When you register your **new harbinger** title—purchased in any format, from any source—you get access to benefits like the following:

- Downloadable accessories like printable worksheets and extra content

- Instructional videos and audio files

- Information about updates, corrections, and new editions

Not every title has accessories, but we're adding new material all the time.

Access free accessories in 3 easy steps:

1. Sign in at NewHarbinger.com (or **register** to create an account).

2. Click on **register a book**. Search for your title and click the **register** button when it appears.

3. Click on the **book cover or title** to go to its details page. Click on **accessories** to view and access files.

That's all there is to it!

If you need help, visit:

NewHarbinger.com/accessories

new harbinger
CELEBRATING
40 YEARS